AF541163

CURRENT SCENARIO IN EDUCATION SYSTEM

CURRENT SCENARIO IN EDUCATION SYSTEM

Edited by
Dr. S.K. Panneer Selvam
Assistant Professor
Department of Education
Bharathidasan University
Tiruchirappalli
Tamil Nadu
(India)

DISCOVERY PUBLISHING HOUSE PVT. LTD.
NEW DELHI-110 002

Published by:
Tilak Wasan

DISCOVERY PUBLISHING HOUSE PVT. LTD.
4383/4B, Ansari Road, Darya Ganj
New Delhi-110 002 (India)
Phone : +91-11-23279245, 43596064-65
Fax : +91-11-23253475
E-mail : parul.wasan@gmail.com
discoverypublishinghouse@gmail.com
web : www.discoverypublishinggroup.com

***First Edition:* 2012**

ISBN: 978-93-5056-074-7

Current Scenario in Education System

Printed at:
Shree Balaji Art Press
Delhi

PREFACE

The book highlights the educational process, which opens up new perspective and warrants the adoption of new strategies for achieving better research. The traditional approaches focussed mainly content and methodology from a teacher- centered point of view, ignoring crucial student factors which profoundly affect his performance. Teachers and educational authorities were dismayed and puzzled to find students performing poorly in spite of good methods and content. This led to the search and study of other factors that influence the student's learning and performance and a lot of research work was undertaken in this direction. The influence of other extraneous factors such as gender, school environment, parent's education, attitude of teachers and these traits has also been thoroughly examined. The researchers have adjusted well-proven methods, techniques and tools have presented as extenuative study of current literature in the field, have collected necessary data carefully and have drawn valid conclusions. The findings of each study, its implications and areas for further study have been clearly presented. These findings will creator awareness among teachers, administrators and parents of the multi-dimensional nature of the students personality and the educational process and will in turn pave the way for a lot of change and reforms in all areas of education. In sum, this book will prove to be an invaluable guide to all those aspirants who want to take up educational research by providing good models of research work and presentation.

Issues relating to quality education such as quality control. Quality upgradation and quality substance has been critically examined. The new role of teachers as facilitators of learning, preparation of self-learning materials and the development of meta-cognitive skills (learning how to learn and monitoring learning) are some of the important topics that have been discussed at length. The exploitation of modern technology for distance education through e-Learning, satellite campuses, tele-conferencing, audio-conferencing, e-mail, FAX etc. has been discussed. The development of INSAT, EDUSAT etc. and their use in distance education have been explained. Thus the book opens up a fascinating field of study for the researcher administrator and the teachers motivating them for further exploration. The State Universities will have to obtain the State Governments concurrence to give permanency to the posts created for permanent positions, especially under earlier plans, if not done already. The University/State Government must take suitable steps. The State Governments concurrence will also be required for the core faculty sanctioned for a new Department. As far as new Departments are concerned, the post of one Reader and one Lecturer will be sanctioned in addition to the provision of grants under the salary component. It will be the responsibility of the concerned University to provide non-teaching administrative/ office staff, accommodation, furniture and other infrastructure facilities; the Department will need to explore other sources for raising funds in addition to the UGC assistance. Conducting self-financing programmes/courses is essential for the sustainability of the Department. A separate fund is created from the resources generated by the Department, to be utilised for the activities of the Department. A separate budget is maintained for the Department operating with the UGC and State Government grants. This edition is mainly a sum total of works and the findings are goes to Benjamin Ngwudike, Jackson State University, Jackson, Mississippi and Mahmoud AL-Ajlouni and Abdulnaser Jaradat Assistant Professors, Irbid National University, Irbid Jordan and Salah Athamneh Assistant Professor, Deptt. Humanities Jordan University of Science and technology, Irbid, Jordan and jesu´ s marti´nez-fri´ as, Centre for Astrobiology, Madrid,

Spain and UNCSTD, Geneva, Switzerland and Sivakumar and Ponraj, Dcpartment of Education, Annamalai University, Chidambaram for helping this book making. The originality of this edition owes to the originality of the contributed by their valuable works. As an editor I acknowledged all the contributors.

Editors

CONTENTS

CHAPTER

Current Scenario in Higher Education

The opportunity to introduce the Extension Dimension in Universities was taken when the National Adult Education Programme (NAEP) was announced by the Government of India in 1978. Then Centers/ Departments for Adult and Continuing Education were set up in Universities. Thereafter, the Adult Education Programme as Point 16 of the 20-Point Programme of the Government of India was introduced (1983-1989) followed by the Area-based Approach Programme (1989-1992) and the Total Literacy Campaign (1992-1997) of the National Literacy Mission. In the Ninth Plan the UGC continued the Adult and Continuing Education Programme in a manner that facilitated the Centers/Departments of Adult and Continuing Education and Extension to cast their own Plan of Action for the Extension Dimension specific to their own University.

In all, the programmes introduced by the UGC from time to time, the main focus has been on Adult Literacy, Post-literacy and field outreach programmes. Attention was given in the Ninth Plan to Adult and Continuing Education for university groups, groups that had passed the university system but had a need to return and to groups which did not have access to the university system.

In the Ninth Plan, the UGC has implemented the schemes under its Non-formal Education Bureau. As evidenced from the UGC's vision and strategy for the X Plan, the scheme will continue to be operationalised by UGC under the Non-formal Education Bureau. In order to ensure continuity, the UGC has already released grants to Departments for the years 2002-2003 and 2003-04.

Now as the guidelines for the Tenth Plan period are being cast it is essential that the current situation, internationally and nationally, be considered. It is well known that the impact of globalisation has placed new demands on the education system. Transformation with rapid change is taking place everywhere. The student and youth have to be prepared by the university to adopt change and learn new skills in accordance with the new demands of the world of work. In other words, the university system has to prepare the student to be a life long learner. Then only will the student be able to sustain his knowledge and skills at an international bench mark level?

Further private universities are being setup and international universities will soon be entering the country. Also, Information and Communication Technology (ICT) is being more frequently used in the field of learning. On-line learning and e-Learning will soon become a regular feature of university courses. It is, therefore, essential that the university system and specially the Departments of Adult and Continuing Education and Extension begin to interact and collaborate with the private sector. Secondly, e-Learning and the on-line mode for the conduct of courses are utilized for continuing education to cater to the needs of various sections of society including professionals.

While universities have to enhance student employability skills through a formal system, on the other hand, the non-formal stream of education is being developed by the Ministry of Human Resource Development for reaching education to the unreached. There is a rapid growth of the National Institute of Open Schooling and State Open Schools and improvisation of quality teaching through the development of a momentum in Sarva Shiksha Abhiyan (SSA) under the Education for All programme. Universities also have to integrate formal and non-formal education by opening their doors to adult learners for life long learning programmes and by making the University an adult learner friendly institution. (Refer' Cape Town Statement on Characteristic Elements of a Life long Learning Higher Education Institution, January 2001).

The Departments, will, therefore, have to play a more dynamic role and move from the periphery to the centre stage of the university system and to ensure this the Advisory Committees overseeing the work of the Department need to play a more pro-active role. The Departments also have to play a major role in the development of the human resource expertise in the subject of Adult, Continuing Education, Extension and Field Outreach.

At present, there are 73 Departments/Centers working in the country. As visualized earlier in the Ninth Plan, all Universities are to establish a Department for institutionalizing extension and for meeting the current demands of adult and continuing education in their respective areas of operation.

Thrusts

The thrusts for the Tenth Plan Period are therefore projected taking the current scenario into account. These thrusts are:

(*i*) the acceptance of the philosophy of continuing education as a part of total education programme of the institution;

(*ii*) integration between formal and non-formal education and out of school learning processes;

(*iii*) reaching out to the larger sections of adults through the university system and specially deprived groups for the purpose of equalization of educational opportunities;

(*iv*) enrichment of the learning process of faculty and students through exposure to community needs, problems, issues and reaching out to socio-economic and cultural groups;

(*v*) attending to major issues relating to the National Literacy Mission, bonded labour, child-labour, street children, health conditions and issues on drugs and AIDS / HIV, nutrition, sanitation, environmental issues, gender issues with stress on gender equity, human rights education, consumer rights issues, communal harmony and cultural integration, self-employment generation and use of technology appropriate to the society;

(*vi*) development of the discipline of Andragogy / Adult and Continuing Education and Extension;

(*vii*) research for the development of theory and conduct of action research/operational research;

(*viii*) introduction of courses offered on campus, off campus, on-line and through e-Learning;

(*ix*) development of courses linked specifically to business and industry which would include work ethics, work culture and preparation for the changing world of work;

(*x*) development of a range of credit courses at the undergraduate and postgraduate levels leading to an Associate degree in Continuing Education and;

(*xi*) Extension and Field Outreach to focus on

- continuing education programmes at the grassroots level through the CECs of the National Literacy Mission and through the National Institute of Open Schooling and State Open Schools;
- communal harmony and peace education;
- human rights and rights of vulnerable groups;
- environmental issues;
- panchayats and development issues;
- health education for the community and through the Health Care Centre of the university;
- women so empowerment and;
- social issues and gender issues.

(*xii*) initiating change in the policies and procedures of the university so as to make the university courses more accessible to the adult learner; and (*xiii*) establishing a new relationship with government organizations NGOs, Civil Societies, NGO networks and other professional bodies to address social issues.

Target Groups

The major target groups for the Tenth Plan period shall be:

(*i*) Groups / students in the colleges and university system;

(*ii*) Groups who have passed out of the university system and need to return for up gradation or for the acquisition of new skills. These could include groups from industry and services;

(*iii*) Groups who are already in service or the underemployed or the unemployed who need to enhancc their employability;

(*iv*) Groups which would normally not be entrants into the university system;

(*v*) Women, SC/ST, disadvantaged groups, street children, bonded labour, child workers, etc;

(*vi*) Neo-literates, CE learners, Out of school youth; and

(*vii*) Senior citizens.

Programmes and Activities

It is suggested that the following programmes be conducted in order to cater to the needs of the different target groups. Departments can formulate the proposals by keeping the following programmes in mind.

Developing the discipline of Andragogy / Adult Education and Continuing Education through academic programmes and courses such as:

- Foundation Courses;
- Certificate and Diploma Courses;
- Undergraduate, postgraduate, M.Phil, Ph.D., optional/regular courses;
- Courses integrated with different degrees such as B.Ed., M.Ed. and professional degrees;

- Projects related to continuing education and extension and field outreach in-built into a discipline of studies; and
- Conduct of inter-disciplinary research in Adult, Continuing Education and Extension.

Vocational Career-oriented Courses/Programmes

- Courses and programmes for people at different socio-economic and educational levels for the acquisition of marketable vocational skills according to the needs and demands of urban and rural, local, national and international markets;
- Continuing education courses for the students and out of school youth;
- Courses related to the electronic media, multi media, computer applications, etc. to receive special focus;
- Apprenticeship, internship, training programmes with industry and business;
- Courses specially focussing on the demands of the changing world of work;
- Para-professional courses for knowledge and skill updates; and
- Career guidance for the university and college students.

Leadership and Human Resource Development

- Programmes for developing the potentialities of students and out of school youth, particularly of the girl students and women; and
- Training of elected representatives of local, self-government, self-help groups and persons from community based organizations, NGOs, under-privileged and resource-deprived communities.

Social and Citizenship Role Awareness Programmes

For increasing knowledge, awareness and functional skills of the student youth and out of school youth in areas such as environment food, shelter, health, family welfare, etc. which affect them.

Resource Support Programmes

- Programmes to support and evaluate TLC, PLP, CE, Sarva Shiksha Abhiyan, women so empowerment, etc. in collaboration with or for the NLM, State Literacy Mission (SLM) Zilla Sakisharta Samiti (ZSS), Centers for Women so Studies, Population Education Centers, Open Universities, People's Organizations, Community-based Organizations, Civil Societies and others.
- Special programmes for indigenous populations, aboriginals, slum dwellers, tribals and other vulnerable sections of society.

Equivalency Programmes

Parallel programmes offered by the Non-Formal Education Sector of the Ministry of Human Resource Development of the State and Centre, Open Schools, Institutes, etc. may be facilitated, developed and expanded.

Academic Credit

The work of the students involved in adult education, continuing education, extension and field outreach work should be considered for academic credit in addition to or as a part of their regular course of studies. For determining academic credits, standards may be evolved and adopted. To illustrate:

- Projects related to extension/field outreach within a discipline at the undergraduate or postgraduate level;
- Field work in respect of a subject of study;
- Participation in literacy, post-literacy, continuing education, population education and non-formal education programmes;
- Participation in programmes for enhancing employability and technology skills;

- Any other activity approved for the purpose by the University Authority with the approval of the Commission.

Each University will have to determine the measures of weight age and the evaluation process for the award of an academic credit.

ROLE AND FUNCTIONS OF THE DEPARTMENT

Teaching, Training and Research

- Teaching courses in Adult and Continuing Education and Extension and Field Outreach;
- Conducting need-based continuing education courses, including online courses on credit or non-credit basis;
- Conducting Orientation and Refresher courses for university and college teachers with the Academic Staff College;
- Undertaking research in the subject;
- To assist in the development of a curriculum for multi-disciplinary programmes;
- To assist in the development of a library in the subject; and
- Training for human resource or skill development for the different target groups.

Catalyst Role

- Acting as a focal agency in the university system for all Extension and Field Outreach Programmes with the involvement of university departments and colleges;
- Serving as a Technical Resource Centre for university's community-based activities; and
- Assessing the needs of the university students and out of university learner for continuing education programmes and career guidance.

Collaborative and Networking Role

The department shall undertake collaborative programmes and network with :

- business and industry;
- university departments;
- N.L.M.A.;
- NGOs, Civil Society, development and government agencies and others; and
- International organizations / universities and agencies, such as, UNESCO, UNICEF, UNDPA, International Council for Adult Education, Asia South Pacific Bureau for Adult Education and similar organizations.

ORGANIZATIONAL ASPECTS

(A) Status of Departments of Adult and Continuing Education, Extension Work and Field Outreach

The IX Plan guidelines have clearly stated the need for the Universities to accord a statutory status to the Departments of Adult, Continuing Education & Extension with amendments, if necessary, in the University Act and Statutes. It was also stated that the Department will have the same status as that of any other teaching department of the university with the core faculty eligible for representation on all the University bodies, like Syndicate / Executive/Management Council, Senate, Academic Council, Standing Committee on Academic Affairs, Board of Studies etc. corresponding to other University teachers. During the X Plan period, the Universities must take suitable action in this regard if such action has not been taken so far. The release of grants for the X Plan will be based on the fulfillment of this condition. In the absence of assurance from the State Govt., no vacant sanctioned post was filled.

The Department of Adult, Continuing Education and Extension and Field Outreach should be headed by Professor/Director/Head of the University Department as per the nomenclature in the University for the Same Position with major responsibilities similar to that of the head of any other teaching department. The University, in accordance with the status of the Department, shall give academic freedom to this Department for the planning and conduct of innovative programmes in Teaching, Research, Extension and Field Outreach.

The faculty of the Department is also eligible for the Unassigned Grant of the UGC available to the university and for the research and other grants of the various UGC schemes for teachers. Departments already in existence shall be eligible for Special Assistance Programmes (SAP) and other such special assistance schemes of the UGC and other national/international agencies

(B) Nomenclature of the Departments

Those Departments which are already known as Departments of Adult, Continuing Education and Extension or any other name approved by the university, may retain the nomenclature. In case of new Departments, they should adopt the nomenclature Departments of Adult, Continuing Education and Extension and Field Outreach (ACEEFO).For the purpose of these guidelines the Departments are referred to as Departments of Adult, Continuing Education, Extension and Field Outreach (ACEE&FO).

(C) Structure

1. At the UGC level The Commission may constitute Expert Committee(s) to examine proposals from universities for financial support under the scheme for fresh induction, advice on policy matters, monitor and review of the Departments completing its tenure, implementation and utilization. The Committee will also be responsible for finalizing consolidated activity-wise and programme-wise annual and action plan for the X Plan, reviewing performance reports from the Departments for further action.
2. At the University level.

   (*i*) ***Advisory Committee***: Since the university is the focus of continuing and extension education and outreach activities, it is necessary to have an Advisory Committee of Adult and Continuing Education and Extension and Field Outreach to oversee various academic and extension field outreach programmes of the university. The Advisory Committee will have members as representatives from: (*a*) the Syndicate/Executive Council/Management Council; (*b*) UGC representative from the concerned Bureau; (*c*) representative of NLMA/SLMA; (*d*) Heads of University Departments/Principals (for Colleges) in concerned areas; (*e*) two three experts in the field; (*f*). Government Departments; and (*g*) NGOs. The membership of the committee may be between 10-12. The Head of Department of Adult and Continuing Education and Extension and Field Outreach will be its Member-Secretary. The Advisory Committee must meet at least twice a year, advise and take steps on courses, curriculum, prepare the annual programme of active ties, look into proper utilization of grants, monitor and review the implementation of the programme with the help of Implementation Committee.

(*ii*) ***Implementation Committee***: In order to facilitate the functioning of the Department, an Implementation Committee, consisting of 4/6 members of the Advisory Committee including 1/2 local members in the areas may be constituted with the Director as the Convenor. The Implementation Committee must meet once in 2 to 3 months. This Committee may also recommend introducing certificate and other short-term courses, suggesting course guest faculty, determining eligibility of students, lay down fee structure and evaluating the programmes.

(*iii*) ***The Board to Advise***: The Department in academic matters including research in the area of ACEE & FO and monitor academic activities, an Academic Board will be constituted as per the university procedure in the form of a Regular Board of Studies.

(D) Faculty and Staff

Head/Director of the Department of Adult Continuing Education, Extension Education and Field Outreach: Each Department will have a Head/Director. The Department will be headed by a Professor/Director, directly responsible to the Vice-Chancellor to whom he/she will report. The Professor/Director of the Department may be selected on part time basis from the disciplines/department of Adult Education/Social Sciences/ Education/Humanities/Management with experience in teaching, research, extension work and field outreach.

The duties of the Professor/Director will be similar to those of Heads of other teaching departments. However, he/she will have the additional responsibility of implementing the UGC guidelines for the scheme. Since extension has to be the focus of the university, the Professor/Director of the Department should possess considerable leadership qualities in continuing and extension education, field outreach programmes.

Faculty

The faculty for the Department of Adult and Continuing Education may be engaged on contract basis or on per lecture basis as per the rates approved by the Commission. All these appointments are within the approved budget.

Secretarial and Non-teaching Technical Staff

The Department will have Secretarial and Non-teaching Technical Staff whose service conditions shall be the same as are applicable to other non-academic staff of the university and they will be eligible to all benefits like pension/CPG/GPF, medical aid, etc.

Field Investigator/Project Assistant

In the Tenth Plan period the Department will be permitted to appoint from the salary component of the UGC grant, additional manpower of 3 to 5 Field Investigators/Project Assistants to implement its programmes.

(*i*) ***Qualifications and Experience***

(*a*) Graduates or Post Graduates with at least one year's office/ field experience in Adult and Continuing Education and Extension and not more than 35 years of age; and

(*b*) Graduates/Post Graduates with a diploma in Adult and Continuing Education & Extension and related fields will be given preference. However, the age of such candidates will not be more than 35 years.

(*ii*) ***Selection Procedure and Appointment***: The advertisement, selection and appointment shall be made by the Department itself after obtaining the University permission. The appointment shall be on a contract basis for the Tenth Plan period only. The candidate will have no claim or right for re-appointment or permanency;

(*iii*) ***Role and Functions***: The Field Investigator/Project Assistant shall carry out academic, administrative and supporting field activities as directed by the Head/Director of the Department;

(*iv*) ***Compensation/Salary***: Field Investigator/Project Assistant shall be entitled to a consolidated amount of:

(*a*) Graduate - minimum of Rs. 4000 per month and Rs. 500 Fixed Travel Allowance; and

(*b*) Post-Graduate minimum of Rs. 6000/- per month and Rs. 500 Fixed Travel Allowance.

(*v*) ***Supervision***: His/Her work will be supervised/monitories by the Head/Director of the Department.

Project Staff on Hiring

No regular or contract staff is permissible under the scheme other than mentioned above. The miscellaneous work of the Department may be got done by outsourcing on hiring basis.

Nodal Universities

The UGC has identified Nodal Universities and also defined their service areas. The Nodal University is a link between the UGC and the universities in the service area. During the Tenth Plan the Nodal Agency System will be continued. However, the Nodal Agencies will be reviewed in the Tenth Plan by the UGC Committee of Experts. New Nodal Agencies may also be considered based on the performance and requirements In addition to the normal responsibilities expected of a Department, each University, being a nodal University, will have the following functions and roles:

(A) Co-ordinating role

- New initiatives, specially in designing courses;
- Disseminating information on innovative programmes; and
- Motivating universities in the service area for strengthening the programme by organizing orientation/training programmes.

(B) Documentation and Dissemination of information

- Documentation Building Archives;
- Updated reference lists of available material for dissemination Books, Journals and Audio-visual materials;
- Use of new technology like Internet, Publishing Newsletter, creating websites; and
- Publications.

(C) Networking at different levels with

- Government programmes;
- Ministries connected with outreach work;
- Official bodies;
- Other universities, professional bodies/training centers; and
- Non-governmental Organisations and their networks, Civil Societies.

(D) Liasioning with UGC, State Government, Vice-Chancellors Committees, State Council for Higher Education, Universities, drawing attention to critical issues; Each Nodal University will convene two meetings of the Departments in its Service Area every year. The meetings are conducted at different universities in the service area by rotation. At least, at one of the meetings every year, a UGC officer is invited for interaction, who should report his / her observations to the UGC Committee of Experts. The departments will be responsible for submitting the annual report and review proforma to their respective Nodal Agency. The Nodal Agency shall be responsible for preparing a comprehensive report of the Departments in its service area and submit the same to UGC; The UGC shall convene a meeting of the Directors of Nodal Agencies, atleast once a year and the Nodal University is expected to be dynamic, rather than routine, if it must fulfill its role and responsibility effectively. For this purpose, the Nodal University must prepare an annual work plan through which it can appraise its performance.

Administrative and Financial Procedures

Re-appropriation within the budget heads upto 10 per cent will be permitted by the UGC with the approval of Vice-Chancellor. If more re-appropriation is needed, the prior approval of the UGC will have to be sought. Non-recurring grants are for a period of five years whereas annual recurring grants are for the particular year for which it has been sanctioned.

Funding Criteria and Pattern of Assistance

It is proposed that every university should set up a Department of ACEE & FO. To begin with in the Tenth Plan, the number of Departments of ACEE & FO would be increased; financial support is given in a flexible manner for an earmarked group of activities. In order to give flexibility to the utilization of grants, the grants will be permitted to be carried forward from year to year till the end of the Plan period. However, these grants will be accountable within the grant norms. In order to give greater stability to the Departments, the salary and benefits for the core staff shall be included in the comprehensive annual budget of the university and in the total Plan proposals of the concerned universities.

The State Universities will have to obtain the State Governments concurrence to give permanency to the posts created for permanent positions, especially under earlier plans, if not done already. The University/State Government must take suitable steps. The State Governments concurrence will also be required for the core faculty sanctioned for a new Department. As far as new Departments are concerned, the post of one Reader and one Lecturer will be sanctioned in addition to the provision of grants under the salary component. It will be the responsibility of the concerned University to provide non-teaching administrative/ office staff, accommodation, furniture and other infrastructure facilities; the Department will need to explore other sources for raising funds in addition to the UGC assistance. Conducting self-financing programmes/courses is essential for the sustainability of the Department. A separate fund is created from the resources generated by the Department, to be utilised for the activities of the Department. A separate budget is maintained for the Department operating with the UGC and State Government grants.

Methods of Teaching and Learning

The variety of teaching and learning methods which is used within a course is an important ingredient in creating a course with interest to students. A course with a large proportion of its teaching taking place in lectures will need to have a high level of intrinsic interest to students to keep them engaged. Over the past few years, a wide range of different teaching and learning methods have been introduced and tested, often with the aim of developing skills which more didactic methods are poorly adapted to do. There is a substantial literature on these methods and on how best to use them. It is not possible here to provide great detail on every possible teaching and learning method, so instead we have focussed on some of the issues which could be considered by course teams when choosing the components of their course. A useful document to refer to is the *Guidelines for Promoting Effective Learning*, produced by the Centre for Research on Learning and Instruction and also available in the TLA Centre.

Lectures

Fifty-minute lectures remain the core teaching method for most undergraduate courses. Their role is best suited to providing an overview of the subject matter and stimulating interest in it, rather than disseminating facts. Lecturing to large classes is a skill which not all staff has acquired and some are not comfortable in this role, and so, where possible, a course organizer is advised to try to spread the lecturing load so as to favour those staff with best skill at it, although freedom of action in this respect is often limited! All students appreciate good quality lectures, and the key ingredients are:

- clear objectives (these can be put in the course handbook, with the lecture summaries, to avoid provision of them being forgotten by individual lecturers);
- clear overhead acetates or slides;
- a paced delivery (the larger the class and/or the more difficult the material the slower this should be);
- appropriate handouts which provide students with complex diagrams or difficult or critical text. This should not be viewed as spoon feeding. It is part of the process of ensuring that students take away the important elements from a lecture, irrespective of how well the lecture was delivered on the day. Good handouts also help to avoid the communication difficulties which can arise in any lecture where large numbers of students are present.

As class enrolments have risen and lecture theatres are used continuously, ease of access by students to the lecturer at the end of a lecture has been reduced. Providing agreed times and places, as soon as possible thereafter, when they can get questions answered is becoming an important issue. A more radical approach to the problems of the large 'performance' lecture is to consider the extent to which some lectures could be removed entirely and replaced by structured exercises (i.e. resource-based learning). To some degree, those students who do not attend lectures follow this path anyway!

Tutorials and Seminars

After the lecture, this is probably the next most widely used teaching method. The distinction between what is a tutorial and what is a seminar is woolly - to some it depends upon size (i.e., 'a 20 person group cannot be a tutorial as it is too big and is therefore a seminar') whereas to others the seminar has a different structure (speaker + audience) and different objectives. This last point - objectives - is certainly the most important issue, and it is probably here that Teaching and Learning Methods and Resources Part III 70 A Manual for Course Organisers most confusion exists in students' minds ('what are tutorials for?'), and sometimes in tutors' minds too. Clarity of objectives is more important for tutorials than for lectures, in that there is general agreement and expectations for lectures whereas there is certainly greater divergence for tutorials.

Much tutorial work is carried out by part-time staff, especially for courses in the first two years, and they too need to be clear about what they are trying to achieve with their students. When asking students about tutorials, the paradoxical finding that they complain about them but ask for more/more frequent tutorials is perhaps closely related to their perception of their need for small group support but lack of clarity about what they should be getting out of what is provided.

Making explicit what students should get out of tutorials can be quite a taxing exercise for the course organiser. A new addition to the tutorial format (at least for most students and staff) is that of electronic tutorials via email, sometimes managed in a WWW forum such as Hyper News. Although rather few courses outside those which are traditionally computer-oriented have experimented with these methods, they hold out promise for those courses where students are difficult to bring together or to enable exchanges between face-to-face sessions. The active nature of the tutorial/ seminar makes it the main source for students to acquire some of the 'personal transferable skills', e.g., in presentation and group work.

Laboratory and Practical Classes

For science subjects, laboratory (lab) work is an essential ingredient of the course and some component of this is generally preserved, even though the amount may fall. In addition to the experience of lab work, students often derive a lot of their contact with staff in the lab setting, and compensation for this may be needed if lab time is significantly reduced. High quality lab work is expensive to provide, and it is important that we are sure that students do indeed gain all that they might from it, especially as the number of students present may have increased, more part-time demonstrators are used, and the frills have been trimmed to cut costs. The balance between fewer but better labs and more but simpler is not always easy to find, but is an important consideration.

Other Teaching Methods

Other methods that may be considered are numerous, including:

- workbooks, diaries, and lab notebooks;
- computer-based methods (see below);
- fieldwork;
- learning in hospital wards and clinics (medical and veterinary);
- independent learning tasks;
- essays, dissertations and projects;
- library searches;
- portfolios;
- posters;
- videos.

Judicious use of them gives students the chance to use a variety of learning techniques so that each gets one or more which suits them best. If you find a possible method but are unsure how best to introduce it to your course, search out someone who has used it and pick their brains. You will probably find that TLA Centre can point you to such people, even if they may not be in the University of Edinburgh.

Students with Disabilities

The University has growing numbers of students with disabilities (e.g. dyslexia) who may present particular challenges to courses with large numbers of students. For example, a profoundly deaf student may be able to follow a lecture with the help of a sign language interpreter, but will not be able to take notes at the same time. A blind student may need special help with practical sessions.

It is not possible to give detailed general advice on making the variety of teaching and learning methods described in this manual accessible to disabled students. However, the kind of support which they are likely to find helpful—e.g. provision of good handouts—often benefit all students. Students with disabilities are students first and foremost, and in many cases of Teaching and Learning A Manual for Course Organisers 71 a little thought and ingenuity on the part of lecturing staff is all that is required in order to allow them full benefit from their classes. The student will often be the best judge of what is needed; at other times the Disability Coordinator will be happy to liaise with staff (Pat Butson, Disability Co-ordinator: 650 6828; Pat.Butson@ed) (*see also chapter 11*).

Computer Supported Learning

Just as it will be the course organiser's responsibility, in consultation with colleagues contributing to the course, to co-ordinate the availability of resources in the Library (books and reprints in the short-term loan collection, for example), all other aspects of resource-based learning will require forward planning with which the course organiser will have to be involved. Various learning technologies (such as computer and multi-media resources) are increasingly being used in support of the learning process, presenting new challenges and opportunities for staff and students. A major resource being used more frequently is the World Wide Web (WWW). An example of its use in presenting information about course content is given in *Case Study 1* at the end of this chapter.

Wholesale importation of computer-based learning (CBL) activities across the curriculum is unlikely to be a wise or desirable move for any course. CBL enthusiasts have been predicting significant gains in quality and efficiency of the teaching and learning process for many years, but the realities have, as yet, been less clear cut. On the other hand, computer-based approaches in education have been subjected to more demanding criteria of evaluation than the more traditional approaches have ever had to face. One of the real benefits of the recent interest in new learning technologies has been the reassessment of our more familiar approaches, which has in itself been useful.

There are undoubtedly areas of the curriculum, however, in which the appropriate and targeted use of learning technologies will be of considerable importance, affording students the opportunity to engage with materials and resources which would otherwise be impossible.

In particular, the confluence of computer and communication technologies suggest exciting possibilities for the use of computer-mediated communication (CMC), in the form of electronic mail or computer conferencing systems, in support of tutorial and group work. While students are facing increasing financial pressures, with the implication that many are functionally in part-time education, the asynchronous communications with teachers and peers which CMC potentially offers can ease conflict between employment and study.

Many subjects, from Fine Art to Neuroanatomy, will benefit from the possibility of networked access to high quality images which may be in short supply, if not completely inaccessible, in the printed form. Computer simulations of practical exercises can allow us to address some of the problems inherent in teaching large classes, provide access to experimental domains which would not otherwise be possible for reasons of cost or personal safety, and circumvent many of the ethical difficulties associated with some areas of research. Many organisations and agencies exist which can provide help to the teacher or course organiser wishing to become involved with the use of IT in the curriculum.

Methods of Teaching and Learning: Case Study

(Source: Tudor Jones, Department of Tropical Animal Health)

The application of World Wide Web (www) technology in the department of tropical animal health.

We have two WWW applications in our department. One supports our teaching of phraseology to undergraduate veterinary students while the other acts as an information resource on our postgraduate courses for both potential and enrolled students.

Phraseology

Phraseology is a very visually-driven subject, especially when taught as part of the veterinary curriculum. It is important that vets are able to recognise the wide variety of forms of the different parasites as well as the different forms of individual parasites. We are currently capitalising on the Web's ability to deliver high quality images that can be integrated with explanatory text as a means of supporting practical classes and lecture topics. We are currently in the process of photographing and then digitising the entire microscope slide collection that the students use in practical classes so that they can repeat or revise any practical session. This is a very important aspect of the web as far as we are concerned as it removes the need to give students access to valuable microscope slides. We are intending to provide lecture notes in hypertext form with links to the slides that were used in the lectures. Our images are all 'mastered' onto photoCD initially and then transferred to our web server in the required format etc. These images are also used in other CAL packages.

We have called our site 'Parasitology OnLine' and it went 'live' in January 1995 but it is still very much under development, especially the organisation and access methods which presently revolves around a timetable structure. We have found that the TABLE format is very useful for presenting images, e.g. the transparencies from lectures can be made to look like 35mm slide mounts and the microscope slide collection can be made to look like a slide tray with glass slides by using the various table format options of Netscape such as cell padding. Later on it is likely that we will provide information such as overhead transparencies in Acrobat format. Our site also has links to other parasitology sites to encourage our students to explore particular aspects of parasitology that interest them. We are also developing feedback forms etc. so that students can contact staff directly with any problems or notify us of any new sites. In this way we hope that this web site will give our students access to a wide range of teaching resources from a centrally accessible facility. You can find 'Parasitology OnLine' on the Veterinary Faculty webserver *http://www.vet.ed.ac.uk/* teaching/Ponline. Access, however, is currently limited to the Edinburgh University domain.

Postgraduate Courses

Most of our postgraduate students come from overseas, often sponsored by international funding agencies, and we need to make sure that information on our courses is readily available to anyone looking for training in any aspect of international animal health and production. With the ever-increasing costs of advertising courses overseas we decided that we should supplement our normal mails hot procedure by placing details of all of our courses on the web. Also all our courses have recently been modularised so students have a wide choice of topics that they can incorporate into their course. Trying to promote those options in a structured way is difficult and expensive using paper as we have 5 courses each one made up of 6-8 modules picked from a list of 44 modules. We hope that by putting all the module options on the web and then creating links between courses and modules that potential students will be better able to navigate through all the options. Also the web lets us include out far more information on individual modules than we could in printed form as well as making sure that our course information is up-to-date. We also envisage that this resource will be used by students to help them make their final module choices once they arrive at Edinburgh. Chapter 8 Methods of Teaching and Learning A Manual for Course Organisers.

The course information is part of a much larger departmental web site that will eventually cover all of our department's activities including publications and research.

REFERENCES

1. Brown, G and Atkins, M (1988) *Effective Teaching in Higher Education*, London, Methuen, p. 245, ISBN 0 416 09082 6 £9.95.
2. Entwistle, N. Thompson, S. and Tait, H (1992) *Guidelines for Promoting Effective Learning in Higher Education*, University of Edinburgh, Centre for Research on Learning and Instruction, p. 106, £5.00 (special price for University staff).
3. Gibbs, G and Habeshaw, T (1989) *Preparing to Teach: An Introduction to Effective Teaching in Higher Education*, Bristol, Technical and Educational Services Ltd. p. 260, ISBN 0 947885 55 2, £9.95.
4. Newble, D and Cannon, R (1991) *A Handbook for Teachers in Universities and Colleges. A Guide to Improving Teaching Methods*, (revised edition) London, Kogan Page, p. 161, ISBN 0 7494 0512 0, £12.95.
5. Race, P and Brown, S (1993) *500 Tips For Tutors*, London, Kogan Page, 130pp, ISBN 0 7494 0987 8, £14.95.
6. Ramsden, P (1992) *Learning to Teach in Higher Education*, London, Routledge, p. 290, ISBN 0 415 06415 5, £12.99.
7. Andresen, L.W. (1994) (Ed) *Lecturing to Large Groups: A Guide to Doing it Less.....but Better* (SEDA Paper 81) Birmingham, Staff and Educational Development Association, p. 94, ISBN 0 946815 58 5.
8. Bligh, D.A. (1972) *What's the Use of Lectures?* (3rd edn.) Harmondsworth: Penguin. p. 256. ISBN 0 14 080321 1
9. Brown, G (1978) *Lecturing and Explaining*, London, Methuen, p. 134, ISBN 0 416 70920 6
10. Cannon, R (1988) *Lecturing*, (HERDSA Green Guide No. 7) Kensington, New South Wales, Higher Education Research and Development Society of Australasia, p. 47, ISBN 0 908557 09 4
11. Gibbs, G (1992) *Lecturing to More Students*, (Teaching More Students, Booklet 2) Polytechnics and Colleges Funding Council, p. 37, ISBN 1 873576 11 3
12. Gibbs, G. Habeshaw, S and Habeshaw, T (1988) *53 Interesting Things to Do in Your Lectures*, (3rd edition) Bristol, Technical and Education Services Ltd. p. 156, ISBN 0 947885 02 1

13. Forster, F. (ed.) (1997) *Support for Part-time Teaching in Higher Education: Case Studies of Practice*, University of Edinburgh, Centre for Teaching, Learning and Assessment in Association with UCoSDA, ISBN 0 9523956 9 X in press.

14. Forster, F. Hounsell, D. and Thompson S. (1995) (eds) *Tutoring and Demonstrating: A Handbook*, University of Edinburgh, Centre for Teaching Learning and Assessment in Association with UCoSDA, Sheffield. p. 96, ISBN 0 9523956 1 4

15. Gibbs, G. Habeshaw, S. and Habeshaw, T. (1988) *53 Interesting Things to Do in your Seminars and Tutorials*, (3rd edition) Bristol, Technical and Educational Services Ltd. p. 136 ISBN 0 947885 07 2, £6.95.

16. Griffiths, S. and Partington, P. (1992) *Enabling Active Learning in Small Groups* (Effective Learning and Teaching in Higher Education, Module 5), Sheffield, Committee of Vice Chancellors and Principles, Universities Staff Development Unit, p. 54.

17. Jaques, D (1991) *Learning in Groups*, (2nd edition). London, Kogan Page, p. 222, ISBN 0 7494 0440 X.

18. LUBIN, J (1987) *Conducting Tutorials* (HERDSA Green Guide No.6) Kensington, New South Wales: Higher Education Research and Development Society of Australia, p. 40, ISBN 0 908557 08 6.

19. Entwistle, N (1992) *The Impact of Teaching on Learning Outcomes in Higher Education: A Literature Review*, Sheffield, Committee of Vice Chancellors and Principles, Universities Staff Development Unit, p. 59.

20. Entwistle, N and Ramsden, P (1983) *Understanding Student Learning*, London, Croom Helm, p. 248, ISBN 0 7099 0921 7.

21. Marton, F. Hounsell, D and Entwistle, N (1997) *The Experience of Learning*, (Revised Edition) Edinburgh, Scottish Academic Press, p. 273, ISBN 7073 0749 X.

22. Richardson, J. Eysenck, M and Warren Piper, D (Eds.) (1987) *Student Learning: Research in Education and Cognitive Psychology*, Milton Keynes, SRHE and Open University Press, p. 228, ISBN 0 335 15600 2.

CHAPTER

Competitive Edge
A Cross-national Examination of Mathematics Achievement

ABSTRACT

The purpose of this chapter was to examine the cross-national performance of fourth- and eighth grade students in mathematics on the Trends in International Mathematics and Science Study (TIMSS) 2003. The TIMSS assessment data were used to identify nations that have a competitive edge in the critical area of mathematics. The Trends in International Mathematics and Science Study (TIMSS) is an ambitious international assessment that provides comparative data on student achievement among participating countries and benchmarking jurisdictions. TIMSS 2003 assessed the mathematics knowledge of more that 360,000 fourth- and eighth-grade students in participating countries in the 2002-2003 school year. Data were collected from students in the countries in the southern hemisphere from September – November, 2002. In countries in the northern hemisphere, data were collected from February – July, 2003. TIMSS 2003 provides an array of data that may be analyzed and used to frame policy guidelines in education, especially in teaching and learning of mathematics. Data analyses portrayed interesting findings. Data from TIMSS 2003 showed that fourth-grade students in Singapore, Hong Kong, Japan, Chinese Taipei, and Belgium-Flemish outperformed the world. At the eighth-grade, Singapore, Korea, Hong Kong, Chinese Taipei, Japan, and Belgium-Flemish outsmarted the world.

The following recommendations, among others, may be of benefit to low performing countries in improving the achievement of their students in mathematics:

1. Low-performing nations should make their teacher education admission, curriculum, graduation, and certification requirements more challenging to teacher education candidates;
2. Teacher education programmes should be designed with a fifth year post certification internship. During the internship, novice teachers will be gradually introduced to the teaching profession. This is obtained in medical and some other health professions. Teaching is as critical as the medical profession;
3. Teacher education systems should establish new teacher induction and support programmes. These induction and support programs should include seminars and workshops, mentoring, observing veteran teachers in classrooms, team teaching, peer interactions, lighter teaching load, and assignment to less challenging classrooms. New teacher induction and support programmes should be used as a means of reducing new teacher attrition rate, thereby increasing teacher retention.

Introduction

The shrinking of the world into a global village and the opening of international borders for free trade had combined to engineer the drive for an unprecedented economic and technological competition among nations. Nations have come to realize that economic and political survival will depend largely on competitive advantage a nation commands over others. Sustaining a competitive edge will be dependent on the availability of a skilled and efficient workforce that a nation has at its disposal.

The abundance of a skilled and efficient workforce at the disposal of a nation is dependent on the quality of students produced through K-12 pipeline, especially in the core area of mathematics and science. Mathematics is the vehicle for producing a skilled workforce needed to sustain a nation's competitive edge in today's global economy. The value-added of mathematics to the quality of a workforce is obvious. Chubb and Moe (1990) stated that mathematics is crucial to the future of sophisticated technology and international competition. As a result of the importance of mathematics and science in international competition, many countries have turned to international assessments in mathematics and science administered by the International Association for the Evaluation of Educational Achievement (IEA) as a way of measuring their future competitive edge.

The IEA is an independent, international cooperative of national research institutions and governmental agencies that is based in Amsterdam, Netherlands. Through its comparative research and assessment projects, the IEA aims to:

1. Provide international benchmarks that may assist policymakers from participating in identifying the comparative strengths and weaknesses of their educational systems;
2. Provide high-quality data that will increase policymakers' understanding of key school- and non-school-based factors that influence teaching and learning in participating countries;
3. Provide high-quality data that will serve as a resource for identifying areas of concern and action, and for preparing and evaluating educational reforms in participating countries;
4. Develop and improve educational systems' capacity to engage in national strategies for educational monitoring and improvement in participating countries; and
5. Contribute to development of the world-wide community of researchers in educational evaluation (IEA, n.d.).

The IEA assessed the mathematics and science performance of fourth- and eighth-grade students in 2003 (Gonzales *et al.*, 2004). The assessments are used for cross-national comparison of mathematics and science achievement of students from participating countries. TIMSS was designed to assess students' mathematics and science achievement midway through elementary school, midway through lower secondary school, and at the end of upper secondary school. Because children start and finish K-12 education at different ages, age and grade level were factors in deciding the students that were tested. Three populations of students were tested. Population 1 consisted of students in a pair of adjacent grades that contained most of 9-year-olds. The adjacent grades were grades 3 and 4 in the U. S. and most of the participating countries, grades 2 and 3, and grades 4 and 5 in some countries (NCES, 1997).

The students tested in population 2 were in a pair of adjacent grades that contained most of 13-year-olds at the time of testing. The adjacent grades were grades 7 and 8 in the U. S. and most of the participating countries, and grade 6 and 7 in a few countries (NCES, 1996).

TIMSS 2003

TIMSS 2003 was the third in a series of mathematics and science assessments conducted by the International Association for the Evaluation of Educational Achievement since 1995. The aim of TIMSS is to improve the teaching and learning of mathematics and science by providing data on student achievement in relation to different types of curricula, instructional practices, and school environments. Additionally, it provides opportunity for participating countries to obtain comparative information about their students' achievement in mathematics and science (Gonzalez *et al*., 2004; Martin, Mullis; Gonzalez, & Chrostowski, 2004; Mullis, Martin, Gonzalez, & Chrostowski, 2004).

TIMSS 2003 assessed the mathematics knowledge of more that 360,000 fourth- and eighth-grade students in participating countries in the 2002-2003 school year. Data were collected from students in the countries in the southern hemisphere from September-November, 2002. In countries in the northern hemisphere, data were collected from March-June, 2003 (IEA, 2004).

Forty-nine countries and the four benchmarking participants (Indiana, United States; the Canadian Provinces of Ontario and

Quebec; and the Basque Country, Spain) participated in TIMSS 2003 assessment at the fourth-grade, eighth-grade, or at both grades. The participating countries were Argentina, Armenia, Australia, Bahrain, Basque Country of Spain, Belgium- Flemish, Botswana, Bulgaria, Chile, Chinese Taipei, Cyprus, Egypt, England, Estonia, Ghana, Hong Kong-SAR, Hungary, Indiana-United States, Indonesia, Iran-Islamic Republic, Israel, Italy, Japan, Jordan, Korea-Republic of, Latvia, Lebanon, Lithuania, Macedonia-Republic of, Malaysia, Moldova-Republic of, Morocco, Netherlands, New Zealand, Norway, Ontario Province-Canada, Palestinian National Authority, Philippines, Quebec Province-Canada, Romania, Russian Federation, Saudi Arabia, Scotland, Serbia, Singapore, Slovak Republic, Slovenia, South Africa, Sweden, Syrian Arab Republic, Tunisia, United States, and Yemen (Gonzalez et al., 2004; Martin *et al*., 2004; Mullis et al., 2004).

The Table that follows shows the average scale scores of fourth-grade students from 25 countries and 3 benchmarking participants in mathematics:

Table 3.1 : Nations' Average Scale Scores in Mathematics (Grade 4)

Nation	Average
Singapore	594
Hong Kong-SAR	575
Japan	565
Chinese Taipei	564
Belgium-Flemish	551
Netherlands	540
Latvia	536
Lithuania	534
Russian Federation	532
England	531
Hungary	529

Nation	Average
United States	518
Cyprus	510
Moldova, Rep. of	504
Italy	503
Australia	499
New Zealand	493
Scotland	490
Slovenia	479
Armenia	456
Norway	451
Iran, Islamic Rep. of	389
Philippines	358
Morocco	347
Tunisia	339
Benchmarking Participants	
Indiana, U. S.	533
Ontario, Canada	511
Quebec, Canada	506
International Average	495

1. Gonzales *et al.* (2004). Highlights from Trends in International Mathematics and Science Study (TIMSS) 2003.
2. Mullis *et al.* (2004). TIMSS 2003 International Mathematics Report: Findings from IEA's Trends in International Mathematics and Science Study at the Fourth and Eighth Grades.

Note: International Average is the average of the averages of the countries and the benchmarking participants.

The Table that follows shows the average scale scores of eighth-grade students from 45 countries and 4 benchmarking participants in mathematics.

Table 3.2 : Nations' Average Scale Scores in Mathematics (Grade 8)

Nation	Average
Singapore	605
Korea, Rep. of	589
Hong Kong-SAR	586
Chinese Taipei	585
Japan	570
Belgium-Flemish	537
Netherlands	536
Estonia	531
Hungary	529
Malaysia	508
Latvia	508
Russian Federation	508
Slovak Republic	508
Australia	505
United States	505
Lithuania	502
Sweden	499
Scotland	498
Israel	496
New Zealand	494
Slovenia	493
Italy	484
Armenia	478
Serbia	477
Bulgaria	476
Romania	475
Norway	461
Moldova, Rep. of	460
Cyprus	459
Macedonia, Rep. of	435

Nation	Average
Lebanon	433
Jordan	424
Iran, Islamic Rep. of	411
Indonesia	411
Tunisia	410
Egypt	406
Bahrain	401
Palestinian N. A.	390
Chile	387
Morocco	387
Philippines	378
Botswana	366
Saudi Arabia	332
Ghana	276
South Africa	264
Benchmarking Participants	
Basque Country, Spain	487
Indiana, U. S.	508
Ontario Province, Canada	521
Quebec Province, Canada	543
International Average	466

Sources:

1. Gonzalez *et al.* (2004). Highlights from Trends in International Mathematics and Science Study (TIMSS) 2003.
2. Mullis *et al.* (2004). TIMSS 2003 International Mathematics Report: Findings from IEA's Trends in International Mathematics and Science Study at the Fourth and Eighth Grades.

Note:

1. International Average is the average of the averages of the countries and the benchmarking participants.
2. Palestinian N. A. is Palestinian National Authority.

Discussion

Student achievement is influenced by many factors, among which are teacher quality, new teacher induction and support, and teacher professional development. A brief survey of education systems in TIMSS participating countries revealed interesting findings in teacher quality, new teacher induction and support programs, and teacher professional development. These findings may be used by policymakers and educators to improve the teaching and learning of mathematics.

Teacher Quality

Teacher quality may be the most important factor that promotes student achievement. Teacher quality is largely related to the rigors of teacher education admission, curriculum, graduation, and certification requirements. The rigor of admission requirements determines the caliber of candidates admitted to teacher education programmes or any program for that matter. The TIMSS high performing countries have rigorous admission requirements. For example, Hong Kong and Japan require teacher candidates to sit for National Subject Area Examination before admission to teacher education programme. In addition to the National Subject Area Examination, some universities in Japan have their own high-stakes examinations which teacher candidates must also take before admission to a teacher education programme. In Korea, teacher candidates are admitted based on their performance on the Scholastic Assessment Test, teaching attitudes, and ethics. In average and low performing TIMSS countries, admission requirements lack the rigor that is obtained in high performing countries. Curriculum, graduation, and certification requirements vary in both high- and low performing TIMSS countries. However, curriculum rigor is more challenging in high-performing countries than in low-performing nations. For example, in Korea teacher candidates are required to take more than 40 credits in their subject areas, and Hong Kong requires prospective teachers to have a minor in mathematics or science.

Teacher Induction and Support

The transition from preservice teacher education to actual classroom teaching can be challenging and difficult. The challenging and difficult situation is a contributing factor for new teacher attrition during the first few years of teaching. As a result, teacher induction and support programmes are used to provide beginning teachers the support needed during the transition from learning to teach to teachers of learners with the aim of reducing the rate of new teacher attrition. Teacher induction and support programs are more structured in TIMSS high-performing countries. For example, in Japan new teachers spend at least 90 days of their first year of teaching in teacher induction activities. The induction activities include in-school and out-of school training, mentoring by veteran teachers, team teaching and observation, and interaction with peers. In addition, new teachers receive support from principals and other instructional staff. The support from principals includes placing new teachers in less challenging classrooms, to grades that are seen as less critical to educational development, and assignment of lighter teaching leads. All these measures are geared toward helping new teachers succeed (Nohara, 1997).

In TIMSS average-and low-performing countries, teacher induction and support programs are less structured, non-mandatory, and less durable unlike in high-performing countries. In average- and low-performing countries, new teachers are placed in classrooms without recourse to how challenging classrooms have become. New teacher assessment may be viewed as fault finding in low-performing countries rather than being an avenue for helping new teachers transition from teacher education to actual classroom teaching.

Teacher Professional Development

New teachers transition from teacher education to classrooms with limited knowledge (Ngwudike, 2001). Therefore, teacher professional development should be seen as part of teacher professional continuum. Wang, Coleman, Coley, and Phelps (2003), found that in TIMSS high performing countries, beginning teacher induction and professional development are required. For example, Australia, England, Japan, and Singapore require new teacher induction, while England, Japan and Korea require professional development. In average performing countries such as the United States, new teacher induction varies and professional development is provided mainly at the district and school level.

Recommendations

The contrast between TIMSS high-and low-performing countries informed the following recommendations that follow:

1. Like TIMSS high-performing countries, low-performing nations should make their teacher education admission, curriculum, graduation, and certification requirements more challenging to teacher education candidates.
2. Teacher education programmes should be designed with a fifth year post certification internship. During the internship, novice teachers will be gradually introduced to the teaching profession. This is obtained in medical and some other health professions. Teaching is as critical as the medical profession.
3. Teacher education systems should establish new teacher induction and support programmes. These induction and support programs should include seminars and workshops, mentoring, observing veteran teachers in classrooms, team teaching, peer interactions, lighter teaching load, and assignment to less challenging classrooms. New teacher induction and support programmes should be used as a means of reducing new teacher attrition rate, thereby increasing teacher retention.
4. Teacher salaries should be higher or at least match the pay in other professions of similar training. This will increase the prestige of the teaching profession, thereby attracting more talented individuals to the profession. Moskowitz & Kennedy (1997) stated that teachers in Japan, Korea, and Chinese Taipei enjoy good pay and high status.

5. Teacher professional development should be viewed as part of a continuum of the teaching profession. Teacher education programs do not adequately prepare beginning teachers for all the challenges to be encountered in the classrooms. Therefore, professional development should serve as a vehicle for bridging that gap. Professional development should be used to introduce teachers to best practices in teaching and learning. Teachers should be a party in designing their professional development activities. The professional development activities should be based on the principles of adult learning and job embedded, and should serve as a mechanism for increasing the competency of teachers by improving their professional skills and dispositions.
6. TIMSS longitudinal data may be used by participating countries to understand the strengths and weaknesses of their education systems. TIMSS provides an opportunity for countries to learn what works better in other education systems while improving the teaching and learning of mathematics and science in their own countries.

Conclusion

The Trends in International Mathematics and Science Study (TIMSS) is an ambitious international assessment that provides comparative data on student achievement among participating countries and benchmarking jurisdictions. TIMSS conducts studies on a cross-national achievement in mathematics and science every four years. TIMSS collects contextual information on how mathematics and science learning takes place in participating countries. The next cycle of assessments will take place in 2011. TIMSS 2003 provide an array of data that may be analyzed and used to frame policy guidelines in education, especially in the teaching and learning of mathematics and science. The analysis of the contextual information collected by TIMSS may be used to understand the context in which the teaching and learning of mathematics and science take place in high and low achieving countries.

REFERENCES

1. Beaton, A. E., Martin, M. O., Mullis, I. V. A., Gonzalez, E. J., Smith, T. A., & Kelly, D. L. (1996). *Science Achievement in the Middle School Years: IEA's Third International Mathematics and Science Study (TIMSS).* Chestnut Hill, MA: TIMSS International Study Center, Boston College.
2. Beaton, A. E., Mullis, I. V. A., Martin, M. O., Gonzalez, E. J., Kelly, D. L., & Smith, T. A., (1998). *Mathematics Achievement in the Middle School Years: IEA's Third International Mathematics and Science Study (TIMSS).* Chestnut Hill, MA: TIMSS International Study Center, Boston College.
3. Chubb, J. E. & Moe, T. M. (1990). *Politics, Markets, and American Schools.* Washington, DC: The Brookings Institution.
4. Gonzales, P., Guzman, J. C., Partelow, P., Pahlke, E., Jocelyn, L., Kastberg, D., & Williams, T. (2004). *Highlights from the Trends in International Mathematics and Science Study (TIMSS) 2003.* Washington, DC: U. S. Government Printing Office. International Association for the Evaluation of Educational Achievement. (2004). Trends in Mathematics and Science Study 2003. TIMSS 2003 (2001-2004). Amsterdam: Author. International Association for the Evaluation of Educational Achievement. (n.d.). Mission Statement. Amsterdam: Author.
5. Martin, M. O., Mullis, I. V. S., Gonzalez, E. J., & Chrostowski, S. J. (2004). *TIMSS 2003 International Science Report: Findings from IEA's Trends in International Mathematics and Science Study at the fourth and eighth grades.* Chestnut Hill, MA: TIMSS & PIRLS Study Center, Lynch School of Education, Boston College.
6. Moskowitz, J., & Kennedy, S. (1997). Teacher Induction in an Era of Educational Reform: The Case of New Zealand. In J. Moskowitz & M. Stephens (Eds.), *From Students of Teaching to Teachers of Students: Teacher Induction Around the Pacific Rim.* Washington, DC: U. S. Department of Education.
7. Mullis, I. V. S., Martin, M. O., Gonzalez, E. J., & Chrostowski, S. J. (2004). *TIMSS 2003 International Mathematics Report: Findings from IEA's Trends in International Mathematics and Science Study at the Fourth and Eighth Grades.* Chestnut Hill: MA: TIMSS & PIRLS International Study Center, Lynch School of Education, Boston College. National Center for Education Statistics. (1996). *Pursuing Excellence: A Study of U. S. Eighth Grade Mathematics and Science Teaching, Learning, Curriculum, and Achievement*

in International Context. Washington, DC: U. S. Government Printing Office. National Center for Education Statistics. (1997). *Pursuing Excellence: A Study of U. S. Fourthgrade Mathematics and Science Achievement in International Context.* Washington, DC: U. S. Government Printing Office.

8. Ngwudike, B. C. (2001). *A Comparative Study of Elementary and Middle School Mathematics Teachers' Professional Development and Classroom Practices.* Ann Arbor, MI: Bell & Howell Information and Learning.
9. Nohara, D. (1997). The Training Years: Teacher Induction in Japan. In J. Moskowitz & M. Stephens (Eds.), *From students of Teaching to Teachers of Students: Teacher Induction Around the Pacific Rim.* Washington, DC: U. S. Department of Education.
10. Wang, A. H., Coleman, A. B., Coley, R. J., & Phelps, R. P. (2003). *Preparing Teachers Around the World.* Princeton, NJ: Educational Testing Service.

Collaboration

Closing the Effective Teaching Gap

Closing the Effective Teaching Gap

Over the last decade, policy and business leaders have come to know what parents have always known: teachers are the largest school-based factor in student achievement. Yet not all schools have equal access to the most effective teachers. High-needs schools that serve large proportions of economically disadvantaged and minority students are more likely to have difficulty recruiting and retaining teachers, particularly in high-demand subjects like math and special education. As a result, they are much more likely to fill those openings with out-of-field, inexperienced, and less well-prepared teachers. Simply put, the student achievement gap is largely explained by an effective teaching gap.

The important question is how we seek to close that gap. Some pundits and policymakers suggest that effective teachers are born, not made—and that the academic ability and personal traits of new recruits are more important for teaching effectiveness than pedagogical training. However, recent studies have shown that teachers are significantly more effective if they are fully prepared when they enter teaching, are certified in the specific field they teach, have higher scores on their licensing tests, have graduated from a more competitive college, have at least two years teaching experience, and are National Board certified. In addition, a new body of research suggests that teaching experience and pedagogical preparation matters for student achievement when teachers have opportunities to learn from their peers in their schools over time. Working conditions seem to matter a great deal for teacher effectiveness — but which ones? In this policy brief, the Center for Teaching Quality (CTQ), in partnership with the Teachers Network, offers a powerful perspective on teaching effectiveness and teacher collaboration. Drawing on surveys and interviews of teachers in urban, high-needs schools as well as a broader research literature, we offer evidence to show that when teachers are given time and tools to collaborate with their peers, they are more likely to teach effectively and more likely to remain in the high-needs schools that need them most.

UNPACKING THE EVIDENCE ON COLLABORATION AND EFFECTIVENESS

About the Teachers Network Study

With the support of the Ford Foundation, the Teachers Network undertook a major national survey of 1,210 teacher leaders, to better understand the role that participation in teacher leadership networks plays in supporting and retaining effective teachers in high-needs urban schools. Follow-up interviews with 29 network participants provided a more nuanced view of ways in which opportunities for collaboration and leadership (within and beyond the classroom) can increase teacher efficacy and effectiveness, and improve the retention of the classroom experts students deserve. The survey sample was drawn from a diverse and accomplished group of pre K-12 teacher leaders in every subject area: 93 per cent were fully state-certified in their subject area and grade level at the time of the survey, and 78 per cent held at least a master's degree. A majority reported that they worked in urban, high-needs schools, where more than 75 per cent of the student body was comprised of low-income or minority students.

The Teachers Network data have some significant limitations, both related to the instruments used and in the fact that subgroups of teachers surveyed were too small to permit meaningful disaggregated analysis.* In this series of briefs and a culminating research report, we have enriched findings from the Teachers Network study with results from CTQ's ongoing research on teacher working conditions and teacher effectiveness. We also provide context from the broader research literature to bear on these pooled data.

Collaborative Teachers are Effective Teachers

Analysis of survey and interview data from teacher leaders provides additional evidence on what existing literature has shown is true of all teachers: that collaboration among teachers paves the way for the spread of effective teaching practices, improved outcomes for the students they teach, and the retention of the most accomplished teachers in high-needs schools.

1. Opportunities for peer learning among teachers build collective expertise. Teacher effectiveness has less to do with individual attributes, and far more to do with the extent to which teachers work with each other and provide collective leadership for their schools and communities. Mentoring has been shown to increase new recruits' pedagogical practices, teaching effectiveness, and retention. However, new studies suggest that teachers *at any experience level* stand to gain from collaborative work. Teachers who have consistent opportunities to work with effective colleagues also improve in their teaching effectiveness. Accomplished teachers instinctively understand that teaching—particularly in a high-needs school—is necessarily a collaborative enterprise, requiring significant peer support and input for success. *Sixty-four per cent of respondents to the Teachers Network survey said they joined their local collaborative networks primarily because they 'wanted a professional community' of other teachers with whom to exchange ideas and best practices for their classrooms.* This hunger for collaborative opportunities

far outstripped any other reason for joining networks—including opportunities for fellowships or other funding, suggestions from their principals. Whether they collaborated in face-to-face meetings (63 per cent) or virtually (76 per cent), most teachers involved in Teachers Network communities were actively engaged in ongoing activities that connected them to other classroom practitioners who could help them 'raise their games.'

Moreover, networked teachers overwhelmingly said that support specifically from peers was important to them for support and for help with their classroom practice. As Figure 4.1 illustrates, a very large majority of respondents cited "other teachers" as their primary supports and sources of information, surpassing even their department chairs, principals or other formal leaders in their schools.

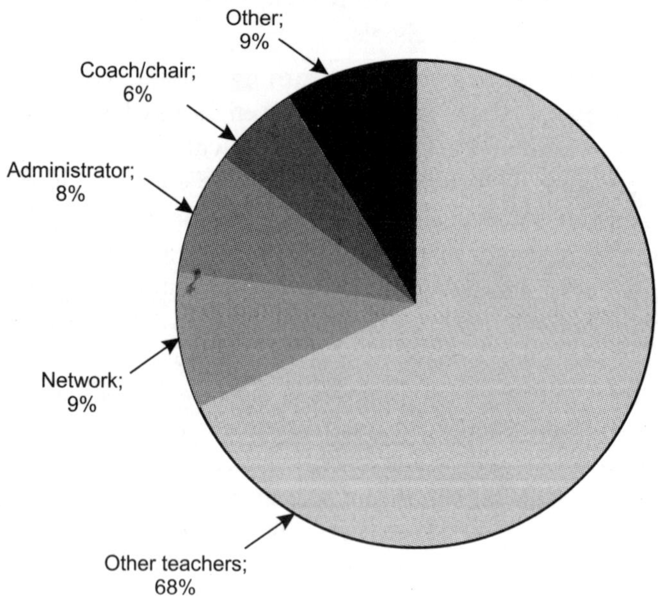

Fig. 4.1a : Sources of support and help for teachers
To whom do you turn for help about teaching?

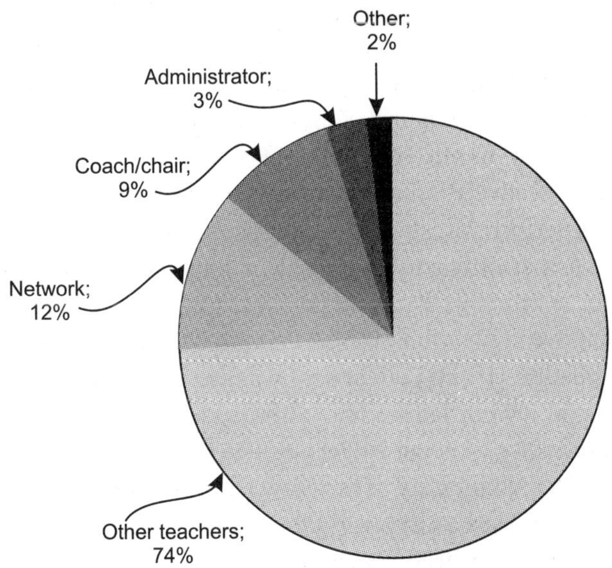

Fig. 4.1b : Sources of support and help for teachers
To whom do you turn for support [as a teacher]?

***Data Source*:** Authors' tabulation of Teachers Network survey data

2. Access to such collective expertise makes teachers more effective in advancing student learning. Collaboration may build the knowledge base among teachers in a school or professional network, adding value to the education students receive. But precisely how much value does that peer learning has, measured in terms of student outcomes? Studies show that students perform better on tests of mathematics and reading when they attend schools characterized by higher levels of teacher collaboration, creating a tipping point for sustained school turnaround. More specifically, a recent study using 11 years of matched teacher and student achievement data was able to examine this relationship even more granularly, by isolating and quantifying this added value brought by collective expertise. Drawing on very sophisticated analyses, the researchers found that peer learning among small groups of teachers seemed to be the most powerful predictor of student achievement over time. Fully 20 per cent of a teacher's 'value

added' effects, as measured by student test score gains, was attributable to shared expertise. *Education Week*, in reporting on this groundbreaking study, concluded, "[T]teachers raise their games when the quality of their colleagues improves." CTQ's own case study research, funded by the Ford Foundation, has surfaced how teachers collectively refine their teaching strategies in order to ensure that low-performing students reached their achievement growth targets. A master teacher within their grade level tested out new ideas for instruction that were generated by the whole team, to be sure that the innovations were effective before introducing them more broadly: [If my colleagues] want to implement something, ...I've said, 'Well, let me try it first and let me see if it [works well]. And if it's a keeper I'll let you all know about it.' Sometimes that knocks the kinks out of the [new lesson or strategy] if just one class tries it versus everyone [in the grade], and that...really saves a lot of time [with trial and error]. Respondents to the Teachers Network survey were also clear about the benefits of their participation in collaborative activities through their local networks, summarized in Figure 4.2 below. Over 90 per cent of the teachers reported that their network participation improved their teaching practice, and over three-fourths feel that it has improved their school overall.

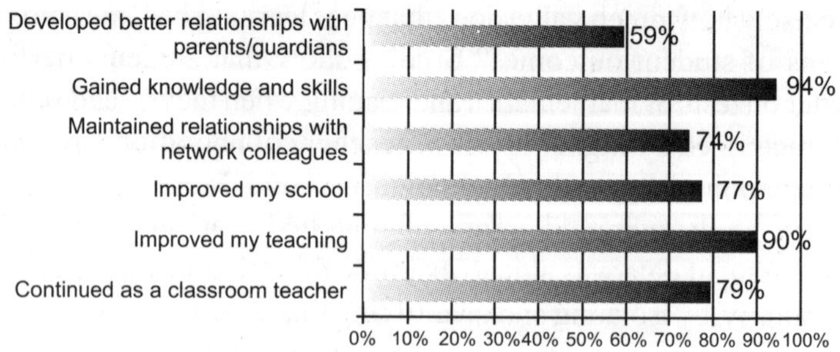

Fig. 4.2 : Teachers Network Survey Responses
"As a result of network participation, I have..."

Data Source: Authors' tabulation of Teachers Network survey data

Of course, not every school nurtures collaborative engagement among teachers. For these teachers, participation in a larger cross-school professional network for teachers, such as those offered by Teachers Network, helped to offset limited opportunities for collaboration in their respective local school communities:

> There was not a [professional] learning community [in my school] and a place where [issues with teaching and learning] could be discussed...comfortably. And being a part of that [Teachers Network community] and being encouraged by them, ...knowing that my problems were not uncommon to their problems, and thinking out solutions about how to fix those problems...has been a wonderful experience, a real learning process for me...as a professional.

For other teachers, having a broader professional network with which to share and collaborate had additional benefits, whether they had opportunities for collaboration within their buildings or not:

> One of the things I love about [my work with other teachers through the network] is that [the discussions are] at the academic and intellectual level of...a master's degree programme. ...I've had to reflect on my classroom, my school, in the context of being a laboratory for [me as] an agent of change. So that's made me really look at what's going on from more of a systematic [and] scholarly approach. ...We're really looking beyond the [current slate of] standardized tests, like what are other impeding variables that may factor in [to why students do or do not experience the learning growth that they should].

In addition, the majority of respondents (59 per cent) also reported that network participation helped them to develop better relationships with their students' parents — an extremely critical piece of the school improvement puzzle. CTQ's recent case studies of three high-needs schools in an urban district suggest that finding ways to engage parents—or in their absence, the resources of the broader community for supporting the school financially or with volunteer assistance—are critical to the success of school improvement plans and student achievement gains. Such expansions of collaboration beyond the classroom walls are also strongly associated with better educational and life outcomes for students in high-needs communities.

Moreover, as Figure 4.2 reveals, almost 80 per cent claimed that their network involvement fueled their intention to stay in teaching. One member of a Teachers Network community put it succinctly, saying, "Teachers stay when they feel that they are supported and that they have good professional relationships [with their colleagues]." In fact, regression analysis of Teachers Network survey data reveals that—controlling for a variety of school factors —colleagues' support was the *only* school culture factor significantly associated with teachers' planned long-term retention. Teachers who planned to stay in the classroom for up to 5 years cited opportunities for professional learning or high standards among staff as most important. But collaboration was by far the dominant factor in retaining these teacher leaders for 10 ($p<.05$) or 15 ($p<.01$) years.

Our analysis of the teacher interviews explicitly uncovered these connections between collaboration, improved effectiveness in the classroom, and retention of those newly more effective teachers in high-needs schools. One teacher claimed: [I]f I had been in [a high-needs] school and just shut my door…, I would've fallen apart. But the fact that I had this very supportive group of people and we were always addressing the issues [that our schools and students faced], and…helping each other work through things [to improve student learning] – that kept me at that school. These findings are hardly unique to the Teachers Network sample. The Center for Teaching Quality's surveys and case studies in other urban districts across the country show that opportunities for meaningful collaboration are one important factor in teachers' decisions to remain at their current schools – or remain in teaching at all.

Making Collaboration Work

The Teachers Network survey did not ask teachers to identify the ways in which collaboration at their schools or in their networks were structured. However, evidence suggests that the structure of collaboration matters to its impacts on teacher effectiveness. However, our on-going studies at CTQ have begun to suggest best practices for collaboration that are most tightly linked to teacher effectiveness. These include:

Scheduling adequate time for collaboration: Whether teachers are trying to collaborate within a grade level group or a subject area department, schedules must be aligned to allow for common planning time. Collaboration rarely 'just happens' in schools; teachers are busy keeping up with their students and often get soloed within their own classrooms. Aligning teachers' schedules to create common planning times sets the tone by showing that school leaders value collaboration. Doing so has been linked to more effective instructional innovation among teachers.

One principal whom we recently interviewed emphasized that the *amount* of time that teachers had together was critical, and recommended at least 90-minute blocks: [Otherwise, teachers wouldn't have] ample time [for collaboration.] ...They wouldn't go in depth in terms of what had worked [with students], what hadn't, what data do we have...to know if this works? The conversations are too pro forma [in shorter meetings]. Teachers in that principal's school strongly agreed. One told us, "Having the time to look back at the [student] data or prepare [your lessons with colleagues in my grade level]...is a big factor [in effective teaching]."

Aligning Collaboration Structures for Both Horizontal and Vertical Collaboration

Traditionally, teachers collaborate horizontally, with teachers in their same grade level or subject area department. Vertical collaboration across grade levels is much more rare, but may be at least as important as horizontal collaborations for allowing teachers to "hand off" knowledge about students' needs to the next teacher – which may be especially important for high-needs students. CTQ's case studies have revealed that teachers and principals find vertical collaboration especially useful for aligning instructional strategies across grade levels for key tested subjects, in order to make targeted achievement growth for reading and math. The structure of collaboration, then, should follow school goals for teaching and learning.

Structuring Collaboration Meetings Formally

Teachers who participate in structured dialogues to analyze student work or solve problems in their schools are more likely to implement positive changes in their teaching practice and improve their students' achievement. One teacher unsurprisingly noted: "It helps to have specific agenda items in mind, at least, when we sit down. ...That way, we stay focused...not going off on a tangent."

Creating an Atmosphere of Mutual Trust

Collaboration—sharing knowledge and ideas—implies risk. Both survey and interview data gathered by CTQ in various urban districts drives home the point that collaboration is difficult to execute without a sense of trust among teachers. Where rifts are deep—between new and more established teachers, opposing teaching philosophies, or clashing individual personalities—teachers report that collaboration becomes less effective: "If you...don't mesh well, then it becomes very difficult to feel successful in a model where you must rely on someone else and their judgement."

Teachers who work in trusting environments have a basis for inquiry and reflection into their own practice, allowing them to take risks, challenge and critique each other, and collectively solve tough problems. And teachers who feel valued by their principals, and believe they are afforded professional respect, are also more likely to stay in teaching and produce whole school improvement (including student achievement gains).

Implications

Human capital decisions have increasingly been a focus of education policy and school reform efforts. Some recent teaching quality reforms have begun to focus on talent management, but not necessarily on teacher development that is fueled by teachers themselves. Evidence from the Teachers Network survey, and in the research literature as a whole, strongly suggests that collaboration and networking among teachers is essential to developing teaching talent among existing staff within schools. Opportunities for collaboration strengthen the skills of new or struggling teachers and can make the best teachers even better.

- Moreover, schools that operate collaboratively tend to be more attractive schools in which to work, assuring that the best teachers will gravitate towards and remain in schools that prioritize collaboration – whatever other challenges they or their students may face.
- To be most effective, though, collaboration should be structured carefully. Principals and other school leaders should allot adequate time for collaboration, organize class schedules to include common planning times that permit horizontal and vertical collaboration, and actively seek to reduce divisions among staff that may prevent open and productive exchanges among teachers.
- Many high-needs schools are likely beset by ineffective teaching. However, many of those ineffective teachers never were sufficiently prepared or supported to succeed in high needs classrooms – and simply removing poor performers will not ensure that effective teachers will be waiting in the wings to replace them. Specific strategies to spread the expertise of the most accomplished teachers may be the key to turning around low performing schools.

Raising the quality of teaching and boosting student achievement in high-needs schools require an intensive focus on a range of working conditions, including effective principals and appropriate teaching assignments. But what may be most important is adequate time to work with colleagues and professional development that focuses on systemic, sustained, and collective study of student work where peers critique and help each other teach more effectively.

About Teachers Network and the Center for Teaching Quality

Teachers Network, a national non-profit organization, leverages the creativity and expertise of a national and international community of outstanding educators to transform public schools into creative learning communities. Over the past three decades, Teachers Network has brought together 1.5 million classroom teachers in over 20 network affiliate communities for professional development that hones both classroom practice and instructional leadership.

The Center for Teaching Quality (CTQ) seeks to improve student learning and advance the teaching profession by cultivating teacher leadership, conducting timely research, and crafting smart policy. Core to CTQ is its own Teacher Leaders Network, a *virtual* community of some of the nation's most expert teachers whose ideas and actions are assembled and spread in order to dramatically improve academic achievement for all students.

REFERENCES

1. Ferguson, R.F. (1991). Paying for Public Education: New Evidence on How and Why Money Matters. *Harvard Journal on Legislation, 28*(2): 465-498.
2. Hanushek, E.A. (1996). *School Resources and Achievement in Maryland.* Baltimore, MD: Maryland State Department of Education; Sanders, W.L. & Rivers, J.C. (1996). *Cumulative and Residual Effects of Teachers on Future Student Academic Achievement.* Knoxville, TN: University of Tennessee Value-added Research and Assessment Center.
3. Rivkin, S.G., Hanushek, E.A. & Kain, J.F. (2005). Teachers, Schools, and Academic Achievement. *Econometrica 73*(2), 417–58.

4. Rock off, J.E. (2004). The Impact of Individual Teachers on Student Achievement: Evidence from Panel Data. *American Economic Review, 94*(2), 247–252.
5. Boyd, D., Lankford, H., Loeb, S., Rock off, J. & Wyckoff, J. (2007). *The Narrowing Gap in New York City Teacher Qualifications and Its Implications for Student Achievement in High-poverty Schools.*
6. Strizek, G. A., Pittsonberger, J. L., Riordan, K. E., Lyter, D. M. & Orlofsky, G. F. (2006). Characteristics of Schools, Districts, Teachers, Principals, and School Libraries in the United States: 2003-04 Schools and Staffing Survey. Washington, DC: US Department of Education, National Center for Education Statistics.
7. Ingersoll, R.M. (1999). The Problem of Underqualified Teachers in American Secondary Schools. *Educational Researcher, 28*(2). Retrieved September 15, 2008 from *http://www.gse.upenn.edu/faculty_research/docs/ER-RMI-1999.*
8. Mayer, D. P., Mullens, J. E., & Moore, M. T. (2002). Monitoring School Quality: An Indicators Report. Washington, DC: National Center for Education Statistics. Retrieved September 15, 2008 from *http://nces.ed.gov/pubs2001/2001030.*
9. Clotfelter, C. T., Ladd, H. F. & Vigdor, J. L. (2007). Teacher Credentials and Student Achievement: Longitudinal Analysis with Student Fixed Effects. *Economics of Education Review, 26,* 673-682.
10. The National Commission on Teaching and America's Future (2002). Unraveling the "Teacher Shortage" Problem: Teacher Retention is the Key. Washington, DC: NCTAF; Quinn, R. J. & Andrews, B. D. (2004, March/April). The Struggles of First-year Teachers: Investigating Support Mechanisms. *The Clearing House, 77*(4), 164-168; Smith, T. M. & Ingersoll, R. M (2003). Does Teacher Mentoring Matter? Unpublished manuscript.
11. Viadero, D. (2009). Top-notch Teachers Found to Affect Peers. *Education Week.* Retrieved September 1, 2009 at *http://www.edweek.org/ew/articles/2009/09/01/03peer.html?tkn*
12. Goddard, Y. & Goddard, R. D. (2007, April). A Theoretical and Empirical Investigation of Teacher Collaboration for School Improvement and Student Achievement in Public Elementary schools. *Teachers College Record, 109*(4), 877-896.
13. Jackson, C. K. & Bruegmann, E. (2009, July). Teaching Students and Teaching Each Other: The Importance of Peer Learning for Teachers. NBER Working Paper 15202. Cambridge, MA: National Bureau of Economic Research.

14. Viadero, D. (2009). Top-notch Teachers Found to Affect Peers. *Education Week.* Retrieved September 1, 2009 *athttp://www.edweek.org/ew/articles/2009/09/01/03peer.html?tkn*

15. Patrikakou, E. N., Weissberg, R. P., Redding, S., & Walberg, H. J. (2005). School-family Partnerships: Dimensions and Recommendations. In E. N. Patrikakou, R. P Weissberg, S. Redding, & H. J. Walberg (Eds.), *School-Family Partnerships for Children's Success,* 189-194. New York.

16. Berry, B., Daughtrey, A. & Montgomery, D. (2009, August). Teaching and Learning Conditions 2009: An interim report.

17. Hillsborough, NC: Center for Teaching Quality.

18. Louis, K. S., Kruse, S. & Marks, H. (1996). School-wide Professional Community. In F. Newman and Associates. *Authentic achievement: Restructuring Schools for Intellectual Quality*, 179-203. San Francisco: Jossey-Bass.

19. Cohen, D. K. & Hill, H. C. (2001). Learning Policy. New Haven, CT: Yale University Press.

20. Bryk, A. S. & Schneider, B. (2002). *Trust in Schools: A Core Resource for Improvement.* New York: Russell Sage Foundation; Tschannen-Moran, M. (2004). *Trust Matters: Leadership for Successful Schools.* San Francisco: Jossey-Bass.

21. Bryk, A. S. & Schneider, B. (2002). *Trust in Schools: A Core Resource for Improvement.* New York: Russell Sage Foundation; Tschannen-Moran, M. (2004). *Trust matters: Leadership for Successful Schools.* San Francisco: Jossey-Bass.

CHAPTER

Teacher Leadership

Leading the Way to Effective Teaching and Learning

A rich literature—both within education circles and in other kinds of labor markets—links teachers' sense of efficacy and collective responsibility to their teaching effectiveness and improved student achievement. Prior research has found that a teacher's self-efficacy as an instructional leader is strongly and positively associated with soliciting parent involvement, communicating positive expectations for student learning, improving instructional practice, and being willing (and able) to innovate successfully in the classroom. Increased opportunities to lead build on one another and translate into increased success for instructional leaders.

Teachers who report more control over the policies in their schools and greater degrees of autonomy in their jobs are more likely to remain in teaching and to feel invested in their careers and schools. However, teachers have few opportunities to lead and influence both policy and programmes. In fact, teaching is a traditionally 'flat' profession, with few opportunities for teachers to advance professionally without leaving the classroom. If teachers are to be 'promoted' within education, such as moving into administration, then they no longer work with students directly. And once they no longer work with students they often lose not only classroom perspective but also credibility with their colleagues as instructional leaders.

In this policy brief, Teachers Network and the Center for Teaching Quality (CTQ) consider the ways in which teacher leadership is key to present-day teaching effectiveness and a healthy future for the teaching profession. We draw on surveys and interviews of teachers in urban, high-needs schools as well as a broader research literature to demonstrate that when teachers are empowered as instructional leaders and decision-makers, students and the public schools they attend will benefit.

Unpacking the Evidence on Teacher Leadership and Effectiveness About the Teachers Network Study

With the support of the Ford Foundation, the Teachers Network undertook a national survey of 1,210 teacher leaders, to better understand the role that participation in teacher leadership networks plays in supporting and retaining effective teachers in high-needs urban schools. Follow-up interviews with 29 network participants provided a more nuanced view of ways in which opportunities for collaboration and leadership (within and beyond the classroom) can increase teacher efficacy and effectiveness, and improve the retention of the classroom experts students deserve. The survey sample was drawn from a diverse and accomplished group of preK-12 teacher leaders in every subject area: 93 per cent were fully state-certified in their subject area and grade level at the time of the survey and 78 per cent held at least a master's degree. A majority reported that they worked in urban, high-needs schools, where more than 75 per cent of the student body was comprised of low-income or minority students.

The Teachers Network data have some significant limitations, both related to the instruments used and the fact that subgroups of teachers surveyed were too small to permit meaningful disaggregated analysis. However, it is a unique data set in that it specifically focuses on the perceptions and career plans of acknowledged teacher leaders in these high-needs schools, many of whom have won teaching awards, been involved with leading teachers' unions or associations, or participated in education research themselves. In this series of briefs and a culminating research report, we have enriched findings from these data with results from CTQ's ongoing research on teacher working conditions and teacher effectiveness, and from the broader research literature.

Leading the Way to Effective Teaching

1. Teachers' leadership and collective expertise are tightly linked to student achievement.

A sophisticated new study has found that schools staffed by credentialed and experienced teachers who work together over an extended time generate the largest student achievement gains. Students of less-experienced teachers who had access to the most accomplished colleagues made the very greatest achievement growth gains.[5] Obviously, these less-experienced teachers had the greatest margin for improvement. But this finding nonetheless implies that the "master" teachers with whom they worked are spreading their expertise among colleagues.

The question is whether teachers have *time* to lead or learn from their peers, either informally or through structured professional development experiences. CTQ's surveys and case studies—and much of the other research in this area—find that they do not, limiting the cultivation of teacher leaders who can spread their expertise to their colleagues.6 The third in this series of CTQ and Teachers Network briefs explores these issues, and their implications, in greater detail. Teachers Network survey respondents joined their professional networks for a broad variety of reasons, including the ability to secure funding for projects in their classrooms or schools and involvement in research or policymaking. (*See Figure 5.1 below.*) Related interview data suggest that involvement in such collaborative leadership work was important to teachers' sense of professional efficacy, and it made them more effective classroom teachers—whether by allowing them to obtain extra resources, learn and practice new skills, or exchange ideas with other practitioners.

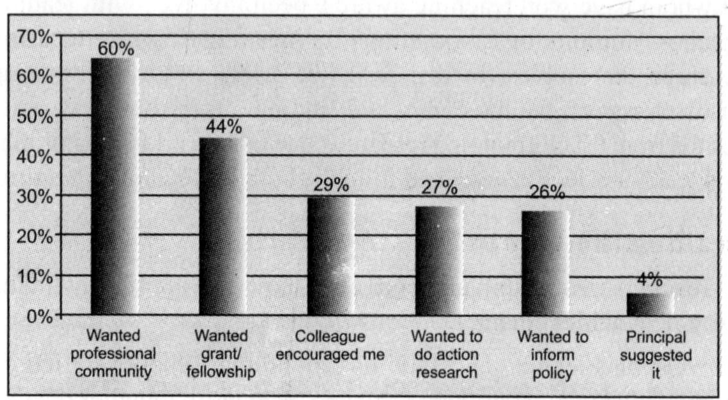

Fig. 5.1 : Teachers' Reported Reasons for Joining Professional Networks

Source: Authors' tabulations of Teachers Network survey data

Interestingly, over a quarter of respondents to the Teachers Network survey indicated that they initially joined a teacher leadership network at a colleague's suggestion. This finding suggests that existing, if informal, professional communities may have given rise to more formal and structured involvements as teacher leaders. While the preliminary survey data cannot tell us who comes first—professional community and collaboration or leadership that drives more effective teaching—the relationship is nonetheless clear and compelling. Are there particular (if hard to measure) attributes or opportunities that make teachers more likely to collaborate and to lead? What skills do teachers learn that make it more likely that they will assume leadership roles within their communities of practice, or in the larger community of educators? We hope that future research can examine these questions more granularly.

2. Teachers search for innovative strategies as instructional and school leaders but are often stifled by prescriptive policies that drive them from the profession. Historically, teachers who have sought innovative or leadership roles within the teaching profession have been limited by occupational norms and organizational structures in their schools. While instructional leadership roles for

teachers have increased of late, the pressure in school cultures for teachers to retain strictly egalitarian working relationships, as well as resistance from administrators, limit the potential of teacher leaders' influence on peers.

Teacher leadership can be problematic—especially in the context of peer review when teachers give critical and high-stakes feedback to their colleagues. However, in other nations (e.g., Japan), lesson studies—where teachers jointly craft specific classroom techniques and critically assess each other's practices—have been found to be drivers of higher student achievement gains. The Teachers Network survey and interviews did not directly solicit information from teachers about any barriers to leadership they encountered. Indeed—contrary to findings elsewhere in the research on teacher leadership – most participants in this study appeared to experience relatively high degrees of freedom to lead, both within their classrooms and in a broader context. Of course, because the study focussed on well-established teacher leaders rather than all classroom teachers, this finding is not surprising.

However, what we did learn from the survey is that many teachers reported receiving a great deal of satisfaction and professional motivation from working as leaders and innovators in their schools—contributing both to their effectiveness and retention. In a recent CTQ study of working conditions and student achievement, one teacher defined the importance of teacher leadership to student learning: [Teacher leadership] to me means taking control of student learning—using the best practices and research-based strategies out there. And if it doesn't work, then what strategy do you try next? It's never an option to say, 'Oh, it didn't work, let's move on.' A member of Teachers Network described the ways in which accomplished practitioners are uniquely well-equipped to design not just appropriate instructional strategies but entire curricula as well: I'm in the profession. I have the expertise. I've studied. I know my students'… needs best. I'm able to fashion instruction according to those needs. So I look to myself more [than to others outside the classroom] as the professional and the expert in the field of curriculum for my students. But policymakers are handing down curriculum to us as teachers as if we do not have the knowledge and skills.

Research shows that when teachers are empowered to function as autonomous professionals and leaders, this builds a sense of professional confidence and pride that feeds effective teaching practice. In fact, both individual and collective teacher leadership self-efficacy have been linked with successful school improvement and reform efforts, by creating a critical mass of empowered experts within the building.[13] These findings are echoed in CTQ's survey results from one large urban district last year, where a plurality of all educators—teachers and administrators alike—agreed that teacher empowerment was the most important school-level factor to student learning.[14] Our case studies have revealed that given the diversity of students entering classrooms, teachers need more tools and opportunities to adapt curriculum and instructional strategies than ever before.

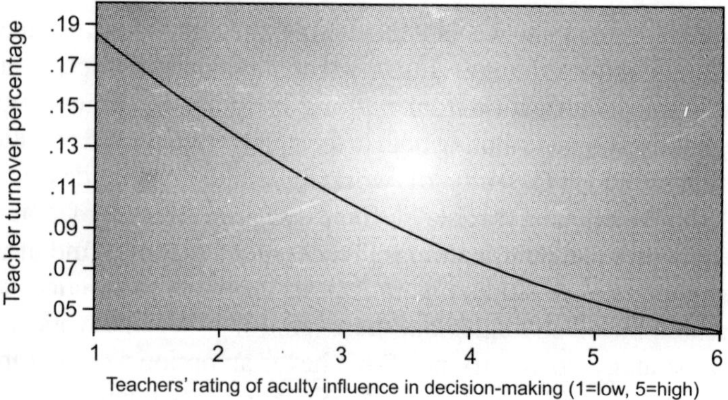

Fig. 5.2 : Effects of Faculty Decision-making Influence on Teacher Turnover

Opportunities for teacher leadership are also critically important to recruiting and retaining the most effective and accomplished teachers. Richard Ingersoll has found a strong relationship between teachers' reports of having influence in school wide decision-making processes and their retention in the profession, illustrated in Figure 5.2 above. Subsequent research focused on reasons for attrition among teachers of math and science—two of the highest-demand subject areas, in which high-needs schools particularly report teacher shortages. This study found that fully one-half of these teachers identified "lack of faculty influence" in decision-making as the reason that they left their former schools or left the profession altogether.

Moreover, teachers newer to the profession are more likely to seek influence in school decision-making and collaborative work with colleagues. Recent research into what will motivate and retain Generation X and Y teachers suggests that opportunities, roles and allocated time for teacher leadership are critically important if public schools are to ensure a strong supply of effective teachers for the future.

3. Teachers identify missing supports for leadership in their schools as barriers to their empowerment and effectiveness. Despite the importance of teacher empowerment, fewer than half (45%) of the respondents in our CTQ survey reported that they played central roles in decision-making in their schools.[19] It is not clear from that survey's data whether this is because administrators did not involve teachers, because teachers lacked time or tools to focus on issues beyond daily demands of their work life, or for other reasons. However, policies and practices adopted by some policymakers or administrators may communicate distrust of teachers' professional leadership, and prevent teachers from searching for and developing and using the approaches their students need.

Micromanaged or scripted instruction: Teachers Network members frequently cited increased reliance on district-adopted scripted curricula or mandated programs as a very basic challenge to their efficacy as instructional leaders:

> [There are a lot of] initiatives and mandates going on [in my school and teachers] are really losing a sense of their own classrooms. [Administrators] are telling you, 'You have to do

this... this is the new strategy or program we're using for writing... or math.' And then [administrators] come in to be sure you are implementing those programmes. ...But I want the freedom to work with my children [and do what's best to meet their needs].

Teachers whose principals, coaches or facilitators did not trust them to go off-script, though, tended to report feeling professionally undermined or burnt out, spoke less positively about formal leadership in their schools, and were less enthusiastic about remaining in their current positions.

Pressures of high-stakes testing and accountability systems: Several Teachers Network interviewees appreciated increased emphasis on professional accountability as a way of strengthening the profession and improving outcomes for students. However, they noted that the ways in which it spurred micromanagement of instruction and curriculum distorted the educational process and made it difficult to teach innovatively and effectively:

Because of the focus on raising scores at my school... our principal's afraid [we won't reach achievement targets], you know. [The principal]... feels that overall things should be controlled [more tightly]. And I think that makes it very challenging [to function professionally and effectively].

Lack of material supports for teacher leadership: Even where principals and schools are supportive of teacher leadership in classrooms and schools, however, this does not guarantee that teachers can take full advantage of those opportunities to lead. When teachers lack the tools, time and materials needed to exercise that instructional leadership fully, they perceive these deficits as implicit challenges to their professionalism as well as barriers to their efficacy. A Teachers Network member reported:

I don't think teachers are treated like professionals.... [W]here teachers are worried about being able to have enough materials, enough books [or other supplies], and there are so many kids in the classroom that they can't devote enough time to...

teaching... content, that's a profound disrespect for the profession. In sum, it is not enough for teachers simply to be invited to the decision-making table as instructional leaders. Teachers also need basic material supports in order to fully realize their potential as teacher leaders and professional experts.

4. Teachers who are empowered to lead within their schools are more likely to remain in the profession.

Teachers Network survey data also suggest that when teachers perceive that their professional leadership is implicitly questioned or limited, they are less likely to remain in the profession. Among former teachers responding to the Teachers Network survey, one-third said that the professional respect accorded to them by parents and students was extremely or quite important to their decisions to leave the classroom. A number of 'stayers' cited similar factors as important to their decisions to remain in their classrooms, suggesting that these two groups of teachers do not have different motivations but rather are prompted to make different career decisions based upon the types of school environments they experience. Thus, schools that offer leadership opportunities for

Table 5.1 : Networked Teachers Take on Leadership Beyond the Classroom

Responsibilities Held in Addition to Teaching	Percentage Reporting This Role
Coach or specialist	25
Instructional leader or department head	38
Administrative responsibilities	19
Union responsibilities	13
Other leadership responsibilities	45
Total holding additional roles	59

Source: Authors' tabulations of Teachers Network survey data. All percentages are rounded to the nearest whole number to simplify reporting.

teachers appear likely to improve not just instructional quality but retention of their most effective teachers—a matter of particular importance for high-needs schools that tend to struggle with recruitment and retention.

Conventional wisdom suggests that some teachers exit the classroom due to a sense of feeling overwhelmed or overworked. But we find that the addition of leadership roles appears to be *less* of a burden on teachers' busy schedules than the addition of routine responsibilities like paperwork and the deadening impact of being micromanaged. As Table 5.1 illustrates, nearly two thirds of teachers responding to the Teachers Network survey reported multiple roles in their schools beyond regular classroom teaching responsibilities, such as school-level administration duties, union leadership roles or work as a department or grade level chair. Holding such teacher leadership roles was associated with significant increases in planned short-run retention over the coming three years ($p<.001$).

Our initial analyses show no differences in career intentions based upon the type of leadership role held. This finding suggests that teacher leadership matters more than the *shape* of that leadership. Indeed, we expect that the preferred modes of leadership likely vary widely among individual teachers, depending upon their skill sets and dispositions.

5. Teacher leadership beyond the classroom walls facilitates the spread of effective teaching practices and breaks down barriers to effective teaching policies. Although teachers tend—in both the Teachers Network interviews and in CTQ's nationwide case studies —to start by defining their leadership as primarily instructional, many also see a role for teacher leadership beyond the classroom. CTQ case studies have surfaced evidence that teachers feel more in control of their work and more effective in guiding student learning when they are able to bridge gaps between what students learn in school and their out-of-school experiences in after-school or summer programs. Parental involvement has been associated with improved academic and non-academic outcomes for students, but engaging families and other community partners is a frequent challenge for

high-needs schools with large populations of disadvantaged or mobile students. Teacher leaders might help to fill that gap by serving as community-school organizers by conducting more aggressive outreach to families, and resolving barriers to their involvement by finding ways to offer translation, transportation or other services. One Teachers Network teacher created just such a programme:

> I did action research on how to better bridge the lines of communication between monolingual teachers and non-English speaking parents — and then created a programme in my school... based on ideas from other teachers [about the professional development they need in this area]. It has made a great deal of difference — and one reason was that I was able to work with and draw on the ideas of other teachers.

Importantly, that teacher's leadership not only directly benefited students and families at the school but also provided vital support to colleagues' work to involve parents. The program could also have served as a best practice model for other schools in that district, spreading the expertise and leadership beyond the walls of a single building. Other teachers interviewed by Teachers Network reported similar 'viral' effects of teacher leadership in sharing best practices and expertise with not only other educators but also with the public and policymakers as well:

> Teachers can make a difference. ...I can write about [what I do in the classroom]... share it with other [teachers], and then I can share with the public. ...I think that... policymakers and the public need to know that whatever they decide [about teaching policies] affects the kids that I teach, it affects me and then therefore it affects [public education], so they need to hear from teachers any way they can.

However, many Teachers Network members expressed clear opinions that teachers' voices were all too often missing from policy debates on teaching and learning, and that those decisions should be more informed by classroom realities in order to be more effective—particularly relating to issues in high-needs schools. One teacher leader, recently named to a state education commission, noted after attending the first meeting:

> Everybody else at the meeting seemed to be part of the status quo, and it was kind of interesting that they didn't have other representatives of people who are in education. I was the only teacher at the table with these education policymakers. And then at that point I thought... *I know why I'm here. I have to be here because people need to hear from teachers who are actually teaching in the inner city, with kids who don't speak English as their primary language and are experiencing school far differently than most policymakers imagine.*

Several teachers also noted that their participation in broader professional networks of teachers was important to their continued involvement as teacher leaders. They saw these networks (both face-to-face and virtual) as essential sounding boards for their work — as ways to test out their ideas and the presentation of evidence before they meet with policymakers: You need the network. You need the relationships, and through this group you begin to establish those relationships. So I have a place to share my voice that's not with just other teachers. And

[my ideas are] not just going to stay in my classroom. I want them to actually go somewhere… so I need to network to learn the skills and to work with the people who have the power [to make a difference for students and their families].

Implications

Research on teacher leadership is still fairly limited. However, our findings here track fairly closely with what we do currently know about the positive relationship between teacher leadership, teacher effectiveness and teacher retention. CTQ's own virtual community, the Teacher Leaders Network, offers a model of policy leadership from the classroom and how such leadership may be an important part of successful school models.

- *Teacher leadership is a critical component of effective teaching and school success:* Accomplished teachers have the most intimate knowledge of both the content they must teach students and the context of the community they serve. Providing opportunities for teachers to serve as instructional leaders within their schools allows them to bring their unique knowledge to bear in meeting student needs and can be particularly helpful in tailoring and streamlining services to students and families in high-needs schools as well as developing policies that can sustain them over time. Transformational school and district leaders who seek out and support the partnership of teacher leaders lay the groundwork for their joint success.
- *Accomplished teachers tend to seek out leadership opportunities but require supports to fulfill their promise as leaders:* Where this leadership can be structured into formal roles, with appropriate time and resources to accomplish the tasks they take on, teacher leaders may be more likely to succeed and less likely to experience frustration and professional burnout. For instance, schools and districts might consider offering half-time releases from teaching responsibilities for teacher leaders. Such hybrid roles would allow teacher leaders to function as peer evaluators and trainers, parent involvement coordinators, education policy advisors to elected or appointed bodies, or special needs facilitators, while keeping at least one foot in the classroom to ground their pedagogical leadership.
- *Expanding leadership roles and advancement opportunities for teachers may be an excellent and cost-effective strategy for retaining the most effective teachers:* Hybrid roles for teacher leaders offer yet another attractive benefit: creating a career ladder in a traditionally flat profession. Accomplished teachers might choose part time leadership roles, or rotating positions that allow them to alternate between full time classroom teaching one year

and educational leadership work in curriculum design, mentoring or other roles the next year. Teacher leaders could be part of peer review programmes and rewards through a differentiated compensation system. Both transformed evaluation and performance pay systems can begin to unlock the current egalitarian culture of schools and promote the spread of teaching expertise from one teacher to another.

- *Professional networks for teachers offer a means by which teacher leadership can be nurtured and expertise can be spread:* Not every school is large enough or well-resourced enough to offer the full range of supports and opportunities that effective teacher leaders may seek. But both in-person and virtual professional networks can help to provide other outlets for leadership and professional learning. These networks can also allow teacher leaders to share best practices for instruction and educational leadership beyond the confines of their building or district, raising the game for teachers in ever-widening circles of professional community.
- *More research needs to be conducted into teacher leadership and how it can be cultivated under different contexts and demands:* We hope that future research can reveal more detailed information about which teachers might be most interested in particular leadership opportunities. Such data might help schools and districts strategically match teachers best suited for particular roles with the schools that most need such assistance, or to design roles as effective retention incentives for their most accomplished teachers.

About Teachers Network and the Center for Teaching Quality

Teachers Network, a national nonprofit organization, leverages the creativity and expertise of a national and international community of outstanding educators to transform public schools into creative learning communities. Over the past three decades, Teachers

Network has brought together 1.5 million classroom teachers in over 20 network affiliate communities for professional development that hones both classroom practice and instructional leadership.

The Center for Teaching Quality (CTQ) grew out of the work of the National Commission on Teaching and America's Future, which established teacher quality as the central school-based factor in students' academic success. CTQ seeks to improve student learning and advance the teaching profession by cultivating teacher leadership, conducting timely research, and crafting smart policy — all in an effort to ensure that every student in America has a qualified, well supported and effective teacher.

REFERENCES

1. Goddard, R., Hoy, W. & Hoy. A. (2000). Collective Teacher Efficacy: Its Meaning, Measure, and Impact on Student Achievement. *American Educational Research Journal, 37*(2), 479-507.
2. Hoover-Dempsey, K. V., Bassler, O. C. & Brissie, J. S. (1992). Parent Efficacy, Teacher Efficacy and Parent Involvement: Explorations in Parent-school Relations. *Journal of Educational Research, 85*, 287-294; Hoover-Dempsey, K. V., Bassler, O. C. & Brissie, J. S. (1987). Parent Involvement: Contributions of Teacher Efficacy, School Socio-economic Status, and Other School Characteristics. *American Educational Research Journal, 24*(3), 417-435; Hoy, A. W. & Spero, R. B. (2005). Changes in Teacher Efficacy During the Early Years of Teaching: A Comparison of Four Measures. *Teaching and Teacher Education, 21*, 343-356; Ross, J. A., Hogaboam-Gray, A., Hannay, L. (1999). Predictors of Teachers' Confidence in Their Ability to Implement Computer-based Instruction. *Journal of Educational Computing Research, 21*(1), 75-97; Tschannen Moran, M., Hoy, A. W., & Hoy, W. K. (1998). Teacher Efficacy: Its Meaning and Measure. *Review of Educational Research, 68*(2), 202-248.
3. Kirkman, B. L. & Rosen, B. (1999). Beyond self-management: Antecedents and Consequences of Team Empowerment. *Academy of Management Journal, 42*, 58-74; Ware, H. & Kitsantas, A., (2007). Teacher and Collective Efficacy Beliefs as Predictors of Professional Commitment. *The Journal of Educational Research, 100*(5), 308-321; Watkins, P. (2005). The

Principal's Role in Attracting, Retaining and Developing New Teachers: Three Strategies for Collaboration and Support. *The Clearing House, 79*(2), 83.

4. Lortie, D. C. (1975). *Schoolteacher: A Sociological Study* (Second ed.). Chicago: The University of Chicago Press.
5. Jackson, C. K. & Bruegmann, E. (2009, July). Teaching Students and Teaching Each Other: The Importance of Peer Learning for Teachers. NBER Working Paper 15202. Cambridge, MA: National Bureau of Economic Research.
6. Smylie, M. A. (2001). Teacher Professional Development in Chicago: Supporting Effective Practice. Chicago: Consortium on Chicago School Research.
7. Little, J. W. (1982). Norms of Collegiality and Experimentation: Workplace Conditions of School Success. *American Educational Research Journal, 19*(3), 325-340; Lortie, D. C. (1975). *Schoolteacher: A Sociological Study.* Chicago: University of Chicago Press; Talbert, J. E. & McLaughlin, M. W. (1996). Teacher Professionalism in Local School Contexts. In J. F. Goodson & A. Hargreaves (Eds.), *Teachers' Professional Lives,* 127-153. Washington, DC: Falmer Press.
8. Bryk, A., Camburn, E & Louis, K. S. (1999). Professional Community in Chicago Elementary Schools: Facilitating Factors and Organizational Consequences. *Educational Administration Quarterly, 35,* 751-781; Louis, K. S., Marks, H. M. & Kruse, S. (1996). Teachers' Professional Community in Restructuring Schools. *American Educational Research Journal, 33*(4), 757-798.
9. Donaldson, M. L., Johnson, S.M., Kirkpatrick, C., Marinell, W., Steele, J., Szczesiul, S. (2008). Angling for Access, Bartering for Change: How Second Stage Teachers Experience Differentiated Roles in Schools. *Teachers College Record, 110*(5).; Humphrey, D. C., Koppich, J. E. & Hough, H. J. (2005, March 3). Sharing the Wealth: National Board Certified Teachers and the Students Who Need Them Most. *Education Policy Analysis Archives, 13*(18). Retrieved June 1, 2005 from *http://epaa.asu.edu/epaa/v13n18/*
10. Lord, B., Cress, K, & Miller, B. (2008). Teacher Leadership in Support of Large-scale Mathematics and Science Education reform. In M. Mangin & S. Stoelinga (Eds.), *Effective Teacher Leadership: Using Research to Inform and Reform.* New York, NY: Teachers College Press; Stoelinga, S. (2008). Leading from Above and Below: Formal and Informal Teacher Leader Roles.

In M. Mangin & S. Stoelinga (Eds.), *Effective Teacher Leadership: Using Research to Inform and Reform.* New York, NY: Teachers College Press.

11. Fernandez, C. (2002). Learning from Japanese Approaches to Professional Development: The Case of Lesson Study. *Journal of Teacher Education, 53*(5), 393-405; Darling-Hammond, L. (2009). *The Flat World and Education: How Our Nation's Commitment to Equity Will Determine Our Nation's Future.* New York: Teachers College Press.
12. Ware, H. & Kitsantas, A. (2007). Teacher and Collective Efficacy Beliefs as Predictors of Professional Commitment. *The Journal of Educational Research, 100*(5), 308-321.
13. Wayne, A. & Youngs, P. (2003). Teacher characteristics and Student Achievement Gains: A Review. *Review of Educational Research, 73*(1), 89-122.
14. Berry, B., Daughtrey, A. & Montgomery, D. (2009, August). Teaching and Learning Conditions 2009: An Interim Report. Hillsborough, NC: Center for Teaching Quality.
15. Ingersoll, R. (2003). *Who Controls Teachers' Work?* Cambridge, MA: Harvard University Press.
16. Ingersoll, R. & Perda, D. (2009). The Mathematics and Science Teacher Shortage: Fact and Myth. Philadelphia: Consortium for Policy Research in Education, University of Pennsylvania.
17. Johnson, S. M. & The Project on the Next Generation of Teachers (2004). *Finders and Keepers: Helping New Teachers Survive and Thrive in Our Schools.* San Francisco: Jossey-Bass; Kardos, S. M., Johnson, S. M. Peske, H. G., Kauffman, D. & Liu, E. (2001). Counting on Colleagues: New Teachers Encounter the Professional Cultures of Their Schools. *Educational Administration Quarterly, 37*(2), 250-290; Peske, H. G., Liu, E, Johnson, S. M. Kauffman, D & Kardos, S. M. (2001). The Next Generation of Teachers: Changing Conceptions of a Career in Teaching. *The Phi Delta Kappan, 83*(4), 34-311.
18. Coggshall, J. G., Ott, A., Behrstock, E. & Lasagna, M. (2009, November). Supporting Teacher Effectiveness: The View from Generation Y. Washington, DC: Learning Point Associates and Public Agenda. Retrieved November 30, 2009 at *http://www.learningpt.org/expertise/educatorquality/genY/index.php*
19. Berry, B., Daughtrey, A. & Montgomery, D. (2009, August). Teaching and Learning Conditions 2009: An Interim Report. Hillsborough, NC: Center for Teaching Quality.

CHAPTER

Methods of Evaluation
Training Techniques

ABSTRACT

The Evaluation of any training programme has certain aims to fulfill. These are concerned with the determination of change in the organizational behaviour and the change needed in the organizational structure. Hence evaluation of any training programme must inform us whether the training programme has been able to deliver the goals and objectives in terms of cost incurred and benefits achieved. The analysis of the information is the concluding part of any evaluation programme. The analysis of data should be summarized and then compared with the data of other training programmes similar nature.

On the basis of these comparisons, problems and strength should be identified which would help the trainer in this future training programmes, to stop short of completion of the training systems design methodology, by avoiding the evaluation, our training effectiveness is reneging on our commitment to our students. The future requires more precise, reliable evaluation strategies, we like to think of training effectiveness evaluation in the same way that we think of surveillance tests in the plant, we perform training effectiveness evaluations to ensure our programmes work effectively.

Keywords: *Training Programme, On–the-Job-Training, Off-the-Job-Training, Training Techniques, Evaluation Methods.*

Introduction

In the modern computer era training has gained the reputation of dynamic concept which needs to be understood in that perspective most of the modern organization which do not respond to the dynamic change that are seen in changed environment may well fail to respond to the needs of organization and people. Hence organization virtually needs to aspire to respond to the change in the environment.

These changes may be concerned with organizational or individual behaviour may be concerned with the structural change. Training is one of most important and effective means of bringing about change in an organization. Training is system which feed the needs. Skills and knowledge of the people working in the organization... these skills and knowledge are acquired to fulfill a specify purpose or goal.

Concept of Training

Training has been defined by a number of scholars and trainers like Change agents. Some of the definitions are as follows: According to Fllippo: "the act of increasing the skills of an employee for doing a particular Job" can be termed as training.

Similarly Steinmetz has observed. "Training is a term process utilizing a systematic and organized procedure by which non-personnel learns technical knowledge and skills for a definite purpose". From the above definitions it can asserted training is a technique concerned with the development of skills and knowledge in particular actor discipline. Training enhances and improves person's skills. Imparts knowledge to change person's attitudes and values towards a particular direction.

William G. Torpey has defined training as "the process of developing skills. Habits. Knowledge and attitudes in employees for the purpose of increasing effectiveness of employees in their present government positions as well as preparing employees for future government positions". The above definition of training is based on assumption that all training is not necessary and all training is not beneficial. Training is a technique which properly focuses and direct towards the achievement of particular goals and objectives of the organization. Hence identification of training needs is first and probably the most important step towards the identification of training techniques.

The process of identifying training needs is carefully thought out programme that needs to be carried out with sensitivity because success of a training programme may be crucial for the survival of the organization.

Objectives of training must be determined to pave way for the assertion of proper techniques of training. Training is imparted to people in organization with certain defined objectives and goals. However it must be remembered that the goals and objectives of organization differ to a great extent. Hence the defined objectives of a training programme should be assessed in the light of the goals of that organization. In 1944. Assheton Committee stated the objectives of training in the following manner: (*a*) It endeavours to produce a civil servant whose precision and clarity in the transaction of business can be taken for granted; (*b*) It helps attuning the civil servant to the task he is called upon to perform in a changing world. It in other words helps him to adjust his outlook and methods to the changing needs of new times; (*c*) It saves the civil servant from becoming a robot like mechanically perfect civil servant. He is made aware of his work and the service that he is required to render to his community; (*d*) It not only enables an individual to perform his current work more efficiently but also fits him for other duties. It develops in him capacity for higher work and greater responsibilities; (*e*) It pays substantial regard to staff moral as latter have to perform tasks of a routine character throughout their lives.

Bhagwan and Bhushan have also identified the following objectives of training:

(*a*) For the performance certain peculiar activities pertaining to the government training plays a significant part;

(*b*) Training helps the employees to become people oriented and inculcates in them respect and regard for general public;

(*c*) It broadens the vision and widens the outlook of the employees by explaining to them to make substantial contribution towards realization;

(*d*) It is vital to a career service. It lists them for advancement which is assured to the employees when they join the government service at young age;

(*e*) It improves the lone and adds to the quality of organization. Since it enhances the efficiency of the employees and develops their capacities. The efficiency and prestige of the department goes up;

(*f*) It fosters homogeneity of out look and esprit de crops in the employees.

Identification of Training Needs

Training is a specialized function. Hence trainer must know exactly what is required from the training programme in accordance to the identified tools framework techniques processes are identified in designing and implementing efficient effective timely and productive training programmes for those who require it. Training needs also determine the nature of training program. Formulation of training program includes those factors that are related to the evaluation of the programme in terms of techniques and skills can be properly considered.

Any training programme must take into consideration three fundamental behavioral aspects: Organization, people, and environment as far as organization are concerned their survival rests on a certain minimum achievement of goals and objectives which are pre defined to customers owners. Employees etc. all these factors are continuously interacting with the organization whose objectives and goals have been formulated so to benefit the members of the organization intermittently.

The second assumption that needs to taken into consideration is the fact that these objectives can be achieved only through harnessing the abilities of its people. Releasing potential and maximizing opportunities for development. In others words. The achievement of objectives and goals can be effectively and effectively achieved only if people within the organization possess adequate skills and abilities. If they do not possess the skills and abilities required. the objectives and goals cannot be achieved effectively and effectively achieved only if they do not possess the skills and abilities. If they do not possess the skills and abilities required. The objectives and goals cannot be achieved effectively and efficiently. Hence proper assessment of the abilities and skills of the employees must be considered before any training programme is being formulated. The third assumption is to assess the capability potential of the employees. The people who are engaged in the accomplishment of goals and objectives. In the new perspective, are capable of new learning. If the employees do not possess the required potential to adapt themselves to the new environment. The chances of training programmes being a success will be doubtful.

The fourth assumption about people is concerned with the level of ability and the desire to learn. Training is all about learning organization basically involves people who make or break organization. The organization should be able to provide adequate opportunities and resources where people are able to learn through training new concepts and techniques of management the assumption is also concerned with matching of achieving organizational goals on one hand and on the other providing attractive learning opportunities. The third assumption basically requires that the programmers of training should be so designed so as to provide learning opportunities that are effective and efficient. The objective of training is fulfilling the individual needs of the employees and that of the organization as well.

The fifth assumption is concerned with the environment variable. In a dynamic situation. Environment continues to put new pressures and demands upon the system even if it is for survival only. Because of liberalization, competition has become severe and public sector as well private sector has to compete with each other in order to stay a viable entity. Hence changes in the environment can no more be overlooked but need to understood and adapted to. The need for training, therefore, becomes inevitable.

Once it is established that need for training is a necessity. The question arises what type of training is required to meet the three challenges. Another important question that comes to mind is whether the training programmed is able to change the pattern of behaviour for which it was trained and how effectiveness is will be measured. Before discussing venous types of techniques of evaluation. A close look at various types of training methods will be locked into. With regard to people working in the organization needs and aspiration of the people must be properly evaluated. Specification of training needs means translating the needs of people into specific needs and achieving those aspirations by training programmers. Basic idea behind this evaluation is to make organization learning organization. According to Senge. Where people continually expand their capacity to create results they truly desire. Where new and expansive paupers are nurtured. Where collective aspiration is set free. And where people are continually learning how to learn together.

Factors Influencing Training Needs

Organizations are complex and dynamic in nature and their effectiveness depends on number of factors. Complexity of organization is again a multifaceted implication of various factors being determined by various environmental factors. Hence the nature of complexity of a given organization needs to be evaluated before determining its training needs. Some of the factors that increase complexity are being discussed keeping in view that all are not determinants of complexity for all organization. Technology in the computer age is being upgraded frequently and hence is the most important factors in increasing the complexity of an organization. structurally as well as behaviourally. According of Frances and Bee, "Technology is changing an ever increasing rate,

Today's state-of-the-art computer is tomorrows junk. Robot assembly pants, Laser printers. "Transplant and genetic surgery—wherever the workplace—whatever the task. There appears to be a technological solution for everything". The technological changes are influencing the basic settings of organization. The technological changes are not only concerned with the structure or gadgets of an organization but these changes also influence the behavioural aspect of the very people who are working in the organization.

However people do not usually change in technology and its environment. Change can be brought about in a smooth manner only through training techniques. Another important factor that needs to be taken into consideration is concerned with social changes that are taking place in the new social environment. For most organization internal compilations are bound to change in the computer age. People from different backgrounds, women. People from diverse nations will from the workforce of modern organizations. With increasing diversity in the culture. The organizations are bound to receive culture shock. Organization with their exiting format will not be in position to absorb this culture shock. The change agent will be playing an important role in providing appropriate training to absorb culture shock.

The third factor that has influenced training needs is related the new role that the government are being asked to play. The governments are being asked to play sensitive role of controlling the business ethical activities on one hand and safeguarding the interests of consumer on the other. In the era of privatization and globalization.

The governments are formulating legislation to facilitate business activity both public and private as well as safeguarding the consumer interest. Thus managers and CEOs need to be acquainted to the new legislation that is being enacted from time to time.

The fourth factor that has influenced the training needs is the emerging competitive market conditions. It may be asserted that the public and private sector, even in monopolistic conditions, have to face competition. The pertinent question is whether the new market situation will force the organization to go in for training as they are going to face new marketing situations in the times to come. Will the new emerging conditions give rise to pressure groups that have henceforth not been seen in the business world? Basically organizations are going to face situations that are the result of competitive markets and development of consumerism. Many of the managers in the public and private sector could not possibly have been oriented towards these new situations. Hence need of training is unavoidable.

The fifth factor influencing the training needs related to internal management of an organization. Internally organizations are going to face new dilemmas and problems. Business needs are fulfilled by the human resources that exist within the framework of internal structure. Any strategic plan which does not take this fact into account is bound to face numerous problems. There will be a continuous pressure on the organization to improve performance. Human resources, like managers, workers, staff, and others, have to be kept up to date in expertise and at the same times need to be motivated to perform better. This is a difficult task which cannot be handled by the staff of the organization. Experts called change agents are required to fulfill the task. Training needs cannot be overlooked because it is an on going process. In addition, Training is now considered a specialized function to be performed by the experts.

Techniques of Training

The object of this chapter is not to discuss various techniques of training. Hence training techniques are being short listed for the purpose of their identification for evaluation purpose. However we would like to throw light on some of modern techniques of training. Some of the training techniques that are often used for reeducation purpose are:

1. On-the-job-training
2. Demonstration
3. Job instruction training

4. Vestibule training
5. Apprenticeship
6. Coaching –Understudy
7. Job rotation
8. Lectures and conferences
9. Syndicate
10. Simulation training
11. Role playing
12. In-basket exercise
13. Management game
14. Sensitivity training
15. Transactional analysis
16. Organization development

A detailed discussion of these techniques can be referred to many text books. Here we would like to discuss some of the training techniques that are considered by the experts as essential for improving the performance of organization in competitive situations. Diversity training is becoming extremely important for the organizations that are complex in nature. The work force of these enterprises is divers in nature. Various diverse groups from different cultural and social background join one institution and thus submerging various cultural into one. The diverse work force has to be trained so as to provide some from of commonality. Various methods are adopted to provide diversity training. According to Fred Lufthansa one method of divers training involves putting trainees into groups based on ethnic origin. Then each group is asked to describe the others and listen to the way its own group is described. Another methods of diversity training has been stated in the following manner. Another widely used approach is diversity board games. Which require the participants to answer questions related to areas such as gender, race cultural differences, age issues, sexual orientation, and disabilities. On the basis of the response, the games players are able to advance on the board or are forced to back up. The objectives of theses types of games are to acquaint the players in a non threatening manner with legal rules and restrictions regarding how to manage members of the diverse groups. The third method of divers training concerned with participant focus on cultural issues such how to interact with personal from other countries. It may be added that many of the training programmers related to diver's work force also use other training programmes.

Methods of Evaluation of Training Programmes

It is extremely important to assess the result of any training programme. The participant must be made aware of the goals and objectives of the training programme and on completion of the training programme, they should be asked about the impact of the concerned training programme. Evaluation of any programme is a difficult task and more so of a training programme. The first step toward evaluation of a training programme is to define the goals and objectives of the training programme. These goals and objectives should be stated in such format so that they can be measured statistically. Also both the trainer and the trainees most be well acquainted with there role in the training programme. In the evaluation of any training programme. The first requirement is to collect valid and reliable data.

The required data can be collected by using the following techniques:

1. Self assessments answer sheets;
2. Question confronted by the trainees;
3. Assessing the collected information and observation; and
4. Final result based on earlier information plus the new data.

Each method of data collection has its advantages and disadvantages. Which need to taken into consideration? The merits and demerits of each method are as follows:

Merits of Self Assessment

1. The cost factor is quite low.
2. Data can easily collect.

3. Time consumption of the trainer and trainee is negligible.
4. Outside interference is completely avoided.
5. Effective relationships develop between the trainees.
6. Well designed answer sheet can produce healthy results.

Demerits of Self Assessment

1. Self assessment is basically self evaluation which can be based of biased responses. The assessment must have enough reliability so as to draw right conclusion in regard to individual assessment.
2. The responses given by the trainees can be based on misrepresentation or misinterpretation of the questions asked. Thus self assessment questions should be small and easy to understand .in addition .no information should be sleeked which will embarrass the trainees.
3. The information provided by the trainees cannot be evaluated in terms of their correctness. All the trainees do not prefer to give the required information lest it may be used against at any point of time.

All these problems can be easily solved. Self assessment is basically adhered to by all the training programmes. However what is important to consider is to make proper effective use of this technique as the trainees provide valuable information which the trainer can use to formulate training strategy.

The second requirement for evaluating a training programme is concerned with the evaluation of the training programme when part of the training programme has been completed. The time factor must be decided before the programme is initiated and the evaluation criteria must be determined before the training programme begins. The first evaluation will give adequate information to the trainers whither the programme moving toward write direction. At the same time trainees will be able to assess the value of the programme in terms of its needs and usefulness. It is extremely important to realize whether the trainees have understood the need and importance of the training programme. As this stage adequate data should be collected from the trainees to make proper evaluation of the training programme. The collect data, interview and questionnaire methods can be most effective. Interviews can be conducted by seeking information face to face, by means of telephone, or by other strategies like group discussions etc. Each of these methods has its own merits and demerits.

Merits of Interviews

1. Face to face interviews ensure some response. If any responses need to be clarified. The trainer can do so instantly. Similarly if the trainees want any clarification, the same can do immediately. This helps in ensuring correct information.
2. As far telephone interviews are concerned though there is lack of personnel touch. The trainee does not feel the pressure of the interviewer to give answers that suit the trainer. The trainer can answer all those question that are complex in nature. These answers have far more validity as the responses are without any pressure.

Demerits of Interviews

1. The interview is a lengthy and costly process as it requires trained and skilled personal to get results that are reliable.
2. Another important drawback is the possibility of the trainer being involved in the interview.
3. Data collected through interview methods may be out of date and hence difficult to interpret.

Merits and Demerits of Questionnaire

Questionnaires in one form or another do appear in all kinds of research and surveys. Hence it is extremely vital that the questionnaire is framed with utmost care so that it measures the variable in exactly the way it has been designed for. Once the initial design has been properly framed, a pre-test must be conducted to find out whether the questions mean the same thing to the trainer and the trainee. If found inappropriate, the questionnaire should be redesigned and a pilot survey should conducted. If found appropriate. Full survey should be conducted and if found inappropriate the questionnaire should be redesigned again. The reliability and validity of the questionnaire should be properly evaluated before going in for full survey.

In regard to collection of data. It may be observed," As with any method of data collection it is vital to plan how the data is to be collected. However with this method, since it does not usually involve the design of some sort of formal survey instrument such as questionnaire. It is all too easy to leap straight in without a plan. This can lead to a considerable waste of time and without a plan. This can lead to a considerable waste of time and even worse the wrong data being collected—so the message is plan and design your desk research in the same way as you would any more formal survey."

Thus whatever technique or method we adopt, the validity and reliability of data must be determined. As a matter of fact the trainer must look at three factors to determine the reliability and validity of the collected data. According to Frances and bee, three key aspects must be considered in any evaluation study. These key aspects are as follows: The first factor is concerned with the internal stability of an evaluation study. It is concerned with how well the study measures what we want or are aiming to find out. This usually involves the adequacy and appropriateness of the measuring tool. The instrument, used. What needs to be? Considered is that whatever instruments we use for the purpose of collecting data, we must make sure that the terminology being used actually measures the variable that we intend to measure. Whether the instrument is interview or questionnaire, the terms must elicit the kind of information that is required. The second factor is concerned with the external validity. It is concerned with the extent that the findings can be applied beyond the group involved in the study. The conclusions drawn on the basis of collocated should not be applicable only to the group that was the basis of collection of data. On the contrary, the collected data should have the reliability and validity to the extent that its conclusions are applicable to other similar situations.

The third factor that needs to be considered is concerned with reliability. The reliability of an evaluation study is the extent to which the results can be replicated, i.e. if the study was repeated the results would be the same. The obvious approach to dealing with this issue is to repeat tests and observations. Also techniques, such as including the same question but in different forms, using multiple observes, etc. can be helpful. The fourth factor that needs to be taken to evaluate training programme is to conduct and determine reaction level of the trainees in respect of the training programme. The reaction criteria are to be determined in terms of open discussion between the trainers, the trainees, and the management. This will give ample opportunity to the management to ascertain whether or not the training programme is achieving the objectives for which it was organized. This evaluation should be conducted half way of the training period.

The reaction criteria tend to inform the trainers whether the training programme is achieving the goals as perceived by the trainers. In other words the trainers come to know the level of happiness and satisfaction of the trainees in regard to the training programme. To ascertain and collect this kind of information, the trainees may be asked to fill a self-complete questionnaire in which the trainees have to choose between ranges of alternatives and answer some of the open ended questions. The self-fulfilled questionnaire seeks information in regard to entry briefing; whether the objectives of the training programme were achievable and how far have they been useful; whether the trainers performance has been satisfactory; and the training methods utility; the mid term evaluation clears the way of the trainers to reframe the training methodology and cater according to the needs of the trainees.

Two fundamental problem need to be assessed in this evaluation process. The first problem is whether information sleeked should or should not be collected in the name of trainee. The evaluation as far as possible be anonymous could give, probably, more accurate information than the information collected in the name of the participant. The second related issue is concerned with the venue where the information questionnaire is filled up by the trainee. It is indeed desirable that the trainee provide information away from the course environment. This mid evaluation can be very helpful in providing a lot of information that is reliable and valid. As a matter of fact mid term evaluation can be very helpful and the cost of collecting such information is not only very low but it also helps the trainees to reframe their training programs accordingly the approach of mid term evaluation allows the trainer to make comparisons between different training programmes that were conducted in other organization or that were conducted by the trainer himself. However reaction criteria of mid term evaluation does generate an enormous amount of data analysis. How much of this data is used by the trainer for readjusting the structure of the training programme depends on the management, trainer, and the participants.

The final step in respect of evaluation of training programmes is to assess whether the basic objectives of the training programme have been achieved or not. In this step cost-effectiveness and cost-benefit techniques need to be utilized to measure the performance. This assessment will demonstrate whether the expected learning that was determined before the training programme was conduced has taken place after the conclusion of the training programme or not. Some of the scholars suggest that before going in for final evaluation, if feasible, one or two, in between, evaluation, can also be conducted. However too many evaluation questionnaires can disrupt the training programme and can create doubts in the minds of trainees towards the effectiveness of the programme in the minds of the trainees can be created. Evaluation of the training programme should be undertaken only for the purpose of feedback and restructuring of the programmes to fulfill the goals and objectives of the training programme.

The basic purpose of any training programme is to improve organizational performance i.e. to assess whether the training program has been able to achieve change that it desired from the training programme. The final evaluation programme must take into factors that might have affected the final outcome, for example, competitor initiatives, general economic conditions, etc. Performance of an organization must be evaluative in terms of the whole unit and not parts of it.

Hence any evaluation of the training programme may not result in perfect achievement of the goals. We should identify the key factors and indicators that can influence the final results of the training programme. The assessment of these factors will help in the analysis of the needs of the concerned organization. In this respect a comparative study should be made in regard to the information collected before the training programme was initiated and after the training programme where changes need to be visualized and thereupon assessed. If possible a comparative study can also be made of the similar training programme conducted in other organization and analyzes the differences in the final results. At the time of collecting the final data, proper monitoring should be assured. All the required data should be collected to make elaborate analysis.

In the final analysis it can be stated that the final evaluation is the most important aspect of the training programme aspect of the training programme in order to find and determine the effectiveness of the training programme. This assessment gives a clear picture of the impact of the training programme. As indicated earlier, clear cut indicators of organizational performance determined before the start of the programme will make measurement of desired change in terms of evaluation much easier to measure.

Conclusion

The Evaluation of any training programme has certain aims to fulfill. These are concerned with the determination of change in the organizational behavior and the change needed in the organizational structure. Hence evaluation of any training programme must inform us whether the training programme has been able to deliver the goals and objectives in terms of cost incurred and benefits achieved. The analysis of the information is the concluding part of any evaluation programme. The analysis of data should be summarized and then compared with the data of other training programmes similar nature. On the basis of these comparisons, problems and strength should be identified which would help the trainer in his future training programmes.

REFERENCES

1. Edwin B. Flippo, *Personal Management*, McGraw Hill, New York, 1984, p.192.
2. Lawrence Steinmitz, "*Age: Unrecognized Enigma of Executive Development*," Management of Personal Quarterly, v.viii, 1968, p. 73
3. William G. Torpey, *Public Personal Management*, 1959, p.154
4. *Assheton Committee Report*, 1944, Para 15.
5. Vishnu Bhagwan and Vidya Bhushan, *Public Administration*, S.Chand & Company, New Delhi, 1998, pp. 393-394.
6. P. Senge, *The Fifth Discipline: The Art and Practice the Learning Organization*, Doubleday, New York, 1990
7. Frances and Roland Bee, *Training Needs Analysis and Evaluation*, University Press (India) Limited, New Delhi, 1994, p. 38.
8. L.M. Prasad, *Principles and Practice of Management*, Sultan Chand & Company, New Delhi, 2001, pp. 497-537.
9. Fred Lufthansa. *Organizational Behaviour*, McGraw Hill, New Delhi, 2002, p. 69.
10. L.M. Prasad, *op. cit.*
11. Tom Boydell and Malcolm Leary, *Identifying Training Needs*, University Press (India), New Delhi, 1996, p. 65.
12. Frances and Roland Bee, *op.cit.*, p.185.
13. Tawfeq Abdalrahman, *Training Basics and Principles*, Cairo, 2007.

ICT in Education

Introduction

Globalization and technological change—processes that have accelerated in tandem over the past fifteen years—have created a new global economy "powered by technology, fueled by information and driven by knowledge."[1] The emergence of this new global economy has serious implications for the nature and purpose of educational institutions. As the half-life of information continues to shrink and access to information continues to grow exponentially, schools cannot remain mere venues for the transmission of a prescribed set of information from teacher to student over a fixed period of time. Rather, schools must promote 'learning to learn,': i.e., the acquisition of knowledge and skills that make possible continuous learning over the lifetime.[2] "The illiterate of the 21st century," according to futurist Alvin Toffler," will not be those who cannot read and write, but those who cannot learn, unlearn, and relearn."

Concerns over educational relevance and quality coexist with the imperative of expanding educational opportunities to those made most vulnerable by globalization—developing countries in general; low-income groups, girls and women, and low-skilled workers in particular. Global changes also put pressure on all groups to constantly acquire and apply new skills. The International Labour Organization defines the requirements for education and training in the new global economy simply as 'Basic Education for All', 'Core Work Skills for All' and 'Lifelong Learning for All'.[3] Information and communication technologies (ICTs)—which include radio and television, as well as newer digital technologies such as computers and the Internet—have been touted as potentially powerful enabling tools for educational change and reform. When used appropriately, different ICTs are said to help expand access to education, strengthen the relevance of education to the increasingly digital workplace, and raise educational quality by, among others, helping make teaching and learning into an engaging, active process connected to real life.

However, the experience of introducing different ICTs in the classroom and other educational settings all over the world over the past several decades suggests that the full realization of the potential educational benefits of ICTs is not automatic. The effective integration of ICTs into the educational system is a complex, multifaceted process that involves not just technology—indeed, given enough initial capital, getting the technology is the easiest part!—but also curriculum and pedagogy, institutional readiness, teacher competencies, and long-term financing, among others.

This primer is intended to help policymakers in developing countries define a framework for the appropriate and effective use of ICTs in their educational systems by first providing a brief overview of the potential benefits of ICT use in education and the ways by which different ICTs have been used in education thus far. Second, it addresses the four broad issues in the use of ICTs in education—effectiveness, cost, equity, and sustainability. The primer concludes with a discussion of five key challenges that policymakers in developing countries must reckon with when making decisions about the integration of ICTs in education, namely, educational policy and planning, infrastructure, capacity building, language and content, and financing.

DEFINITION OF TERMS

What are ICTs and What Types of ICTs are Commonly Used in Education?

ICTs stand for *information and communication technologies* and are defined, for the purposes of this primer, as a "diverse set of technological tools and resources used to communicate, and to create, disseminate, store, and manage information."[4] These technologies include *computers, the Internet, broadcasting technologies (radio and television), and telephony.*

In recent years there has been a groundswell of interest in how computers and the Internet can best be harnessed to improve the efficiency and effectiveness of education at all levels and in both formal and non-formal settings. But ICTs are more than just these technologies; older technologies such as the telephone, radio and television, although now given less attention, have a longer and richer history as instructional tools.[5] For instance, radio and television have for over forty years been used for open and distance learning, although print remains the cheapest, most accessible and therefore most dominant delivery mechanism in both developed and developing countries.[6] The use of computers and the Internet is still in its infancy in developing countries, if these are used at all, due to limited infrastructure and the attendant high costs of access.

Moreover, different technologies are typically used in combination rather than as the sole delivery mechanism. For instance, the Kothmale Community Radio Internet uses both radio broadcasts and computer and Internet technologies to facilitate the sharing of information and provide educational opportunities in a rural community in Sri Lanka.[7] The Open University of the United Kingdom (UKOU), established in 1969 as the first educational institution in the world wholly dedicated to open and distance learning, still relies heavily on print-based materials supplemented by radio, television and, in recent years, online programming.[8] Similarly, the Indira Gandhi National Open University in India combines the use of print, recorded audio and video, broadcast radio and television, and audio conferencing technologies.[9]

What is e-Learning?

Although most commonly associated with higher education and corporate training, e-Learning encompasses learning at all levels, both formal and non-formal, that uses an information network—the Internet, an intranet (LAN) or extranet (WAN)—whether wholly or in part, for course delivery, interaction and/or facilitation. Others prefer the term *online learning. Web-based learning* is a subset of e-Learning and refers to learning using an Internet browser (such as Netscape or Internet Explorer).

What is Blended Learning?

Another term that is gaining currency is blended learning. This refers to learning models that combine traditional classroom practice with e-Learning solutions. For example, students in a traditional class can be assigned both print-based and online materials, have online mentoring sessions with their teacher through chat, and are subscribed to a class email list. Or a Web-based training course can be enhanced by periodic face-to-face instruction. 'Blending' was prompted by the recognition that not all learning is best achieved in an electronically-mediated environment, particularly one that dispenses with a live instructor altogether. Instead, consideration must be given to the subject matter, the learning objectives and outcomes, the characteristics of the learners, and the learning context in order to arrive at the optimum mix of instructional and delivery methods.

What is Open and Distance Learning?

Open and distance learning is defined by the Commonwealth of Learning as "a way of providing learning opportunities that is characterized by the separation of teacher and learner in time or place, or both time and place; learning that is certified in some way by an institution or agency; the use of a variety of media, including print and electronic; two-way communications that allow learners and tutors to interact; the possibility of occasional face-to-face meetings; and a specialized division of labour in the production and delivery of courses."[10]

What is Meant by a Learner-centered Environment?

The National Research Council of the U.S. defines learner-centered environments as those that "pay careful attention to the knowledge, skills, attitudes, and beliefs that learners bring with them to the classroom."[11] The impetus for learner-centeredness derives from a theory of learning called constructivism, which views learning as a process in which individuals 'construct' meaning based on prior knowledge and experience. Experience enables individuals to build mental models or schemas, which in turn provide meaning and organization to subsequent experience. Thus knowledge is not 'out there', independent of the learner and which the learner passively receives; rather, knowledge is created through an active process in which the learner transforms information, constructs hypothesis, and makes decisions using his/her mental models. A form of constructivism called social constructivism also emphasizes the role of the teacher, parents, peers and other community members in helping learners to master concepts that they would not be able to understand on their own. For social constructivists, learning must be active, contextual and social. It is best done in a group setting with the teacher as facilitator or guide.

THE PROMISE OF ICTS IN EDUCATION

For developing countries ICTs have the potential for increasing access to and improving the relevance and quality of education. It thus represents a potentially equalizing strategy for developing countries.

> *[ICTs] greatly facilitate the acquisition and absorption of knowledge, offering developing countries unprecedented opportunities to enhance educational systems, improve policy formulation and execution, and widen the range of opportunities for business and the poor. One of the greatest hardships endured by the poor, and by many others who live in the poorest countries, is their sense of isolation. The new communications technologies promise to reduce that sense of isolation, and to open access to knowledge in ways unimaginable not long ago.*[12]

However, the reality of the Digital Divide—the gap between those who have access to and control of technology and those who do not—means that the introduction and integration of ICTs at different levels and in various types of education will be a most challenging undertaking. Failure to meet the challenge would mean a further widening of the knowledge gap and the deepening of existing economic and social inequalities.

How Can ICTs Help Expand Access to Education?

ICTs are a potentially powerful tool for extending educational opportunities, both formal and non-formal, to previously underserved constituencies—scattered and rural populations, groups traditionally excluded from education due to cultural or social reasons such as ethnic minorities, girls and women, persons with disabilities, and the elderly, as well as all others who for reasons of cost or because of time constraints are unable to enroll on campus.

• ***Anytime, anywhere:*** One defining feature of ICTs is their ability to transcend time and space. ICTs make possible asynchronous learning, or learning characterized by a time lag between the delivery of instruction and its reception by learners. Online course materials, for example, may be accessed 24 hours a day, 7 days a week. ICT-based educational delivery (e.g., educational programming broadcast over radio or television) also dispenses with the need for all learners and the instructor to be in one physical location. Additionally, certain types of ICTs, such as teleconferencing technologies, enable instruction to be received simultaneously by multiple, geographically dispersed learners (i.e., synchronous learning).

• ***Access to remote learning resources:*** Teachers and learners no longer have to rely solely on printed books and other materials in physical media housed in libraries (and available in limited quantities) for their educational needs. With the Internet and the World Wide Web, a wealth of learning materials in almost every subject and in a variety of media can now be accessed from anywhere at anytime of the day and by an unlimited number of people. This is particularly significant for many schools in developing countries, and even some in developed countries, that have limited and outdated library resources. ICTs also facilitate access to resource persons— mentors, experts, researchers, professionals, business leaders, and peers—all over the world.

How Does the Use of ICTs Help Prepare Individuals for the Workplace?

One of the most commonly cited reasons for using ICTs in the classroom has been to better prepare the current generation of students for a workplace where ICTs, particularly computers, the Internet and related technologies, are becoming more and more ubiquitous. Technological literacy, or the ability to use ICTs effectively and efficiently, is thus seen as representing a competitive edge in an increasingly globalizing job market. Technological literacy, however, are not the only skill well-paying jobs in the new global economy will require. EnGauge of the North Central Regional Educational Laboratory (U.S.) has identified what it calls "21st Century Skills," which includes digital age literacy (consisting of functional literacy, visual literacy, scientific literacy, technological literacy, information literacy, cultural literacy, and global awareness), inventive thinking, higher-order thinking and sound reasoning, effective communication, and high productivity.[13] *(See Table 7.1 on next page for a brief explanation of each skill.)*

The potential of ICTs to promote the acquisition of these skills is tied to its use as a tool for raising educational quality, including promoting the shift to a learner-centered environment.

How Can the Use of ICTs Help Improve the Quality of Education?

Improving the quality of education and training is a critical issue, particularly at a time of educational expansion. ICTs can enhance the quality of education in several ways: by increasing learner motivation and engagement, by facilitating the acquisition of basic skills, and by enhancing teacher training.[14] ICTs are also transformational tools which, when used appropriately, can promote the shift to a learner-centered environment.

Table 7.1 : Skills Needed in the Workplace of the Future

Digital Age Literacy	
Functional literacy	Ability to decipher meaning and express ideas in a range of media: this includes the use of images graphics, video, charts and graphs or visual literacy
Scientific literacy	Understanding of both the theoretical and applied aspects of science and mathematics
Technology literacy	Competence in the use of information and communication technologies
Information literacy	Ability to find, evaluate and make appropriate use of information, including via the use of ICTs
Cultural literacy	Appreciation of the diversity of cultures
Gloabal awareness	Understanding of how nations, corporations and communities all over the world are interrelated
Inventive Thinking	
Adaptability	Ability to adapt and manage in a complex, interdependent world
Curiosity	Desire to know
Creativity	Ability to use imagination to create new things
Risk-taking	Ability to take risks
Higher-order Thinking Creative Problem-solving and Logical Thinking that Result in Sound Judgements	
Effective Communication	
Teaming	Ability to work in a team
Collaboration and interpersonal skills	Ability to interact smoothly and work effectively with others
Personal and social responsibility	Be accountable for the way they use ICTs and to team to use ICTs for the public good
Interactive communication	Competence in conveying, transmitting, accessing and understanding information

High Productivity	Ability to prioritise, plan, and manage programmes and projects to achieve the desired results ability to apply what they leam in the classroom to real-life contexts to create relevant, high-quality products

Source: Adapted from EnGauge. North Central Regional Educational Laboratory. Available Online at http://www.ncrel.org/engauge/skills.htm.Accessed 31 May 2002.

Motivating to learn: ICTs such as videos, television and multimedia computer software that combine text, sound, and colourful, moving images can be used to provide challenging and authentic content that will engage the student in the learning process. Interactive radio likewise makes use of sound effects, songs, dramatizations, comic skits, and other performance conventions to compel the students to listen and become involved in the lessons being delivered. More so than any other type of ICT, networked computers with Internet connectivity can increase learner motivation as it combines the media richness and interactivity of other ICTs with the opportunity to connect with real people and to participate in real world events.

Facilitating the acquisition of basic skills: The transmission of basic skills and concepts that are the foundation of higher order thinking skills and creativity can be facilitated by ICTs through drill and practice. Educational television programs such as *Sesame Street* use repetition and reinforcement to teach the alphabet, numbers, colors, shapes and other basic concepts. Most of the early uses of computers were for computer-based learning (also called computer-assisted instruction) that focused on mastery of skills and content through repetition and reinforcement. *(See section below on Computer-based Learning.)*

Enhancing teacher training: ICTs have also been used to improve access to and the quality of teacher training. For example, institutions like the Cyber Teacher Training Center (CTTC) in South Korea are taking advantage of the Internet to provide better teacher professional development opportunities to in-service teachers. The government-funded CTTC, established in 1997, offers self-directed, self-paced Web-based courses for primary and secondary school teachers. Courses include "Computers in the Information Society," Education Reform, and "Future Society and Education." Online tutorials are also offered, with some courses requiring occasional face-to-face meetings.15 In China, large-scale radio and television-based teacher education has for many years been conducted by the China Central Radio and TV University,16 the Shanghai Radio and TV University and many other RTVUs in the country. At Indira Gandhi National Open University, satellite-based one-way video- and two-way audio-conferencing was held in 1996, supplemented by print-materials and recorded video, to train 910 primary school teachers and facilitators from 20 district training institutes in Karnataka State. The teachers interacted with remote lecturers by telephone and fax.[17]

Electronic Tutorials to Enhance Learner Support at Universities Terbuka, Indonesia

Since its establishment in 1984 as the first distance and open learning institution in Indonesia, the Universitas Terbuka (Indonesian Open Learning University) has made great strides in making higher education available to Indonesians, having served more than 400,000 students nationwide in its 14 years of existence. The mandate of Universitas

Terbuka, however, is not only to expand educational opportunity but also to "improve[e] the quality of education and make it more relevant to national development needs."[18] In its effort to address issues of quality in instruction, it has recently introduced the use of the Internet and a combination of facsimile and Internet technologies for student tutorials in 40 of its more than 700 courses on offer. These electronic tutorials are a supplement to more traditional tutorial models—including face-to-face, regular mail, radio and television—already employed by the university.

Two electronic tutorial models are being used: tutorials via email lists, and tutorials via a combination of email and fax messages. In the latter, tutors send email messages to a "fax gateway" which are then received by students as fax messages while student's messages are sent by fax and then converted to email messages to the tutors. While both models allow tutor-student and student-student interaction, the fax/Internet model is the more accessible of the two since fax services in Indonesia are cheaper than Internet access, and do not require students to have basic computing and emailing skills.

These two models were initially piloted over a two-semester period and results revealed low participation rates for both students and tutors. This was due partly to the lack of familiarity and comfort with using the technology and partly to more basic confusion over the purpose of the tutorials. Tutors also claimed that the limited availability of computers, lack of time and low student participation dampened their initial interest in electronic tutorials.

Thus, while Internet and fax technologies have the potential to enhance learning support at Universities Terbuka, practical steps must be taken to improve tutor-to-computer ratios, upgrade the computing and emailing skills of both academic staff and students, more aggressively promote the electronic tutorial model, and not least, collaborate with external institutions to create more Internet access points throughout Indonesia.

Source: Tian Belawati, *et al.* Electronic Tutorials: Indonesian Experience; available from http://www.irrodl.org/content/v3.1/belawati_rn.html; Internet; accessed 7 August 2002.

How Can ICTs Help Transform the Learning Environment into One that is Learner-centered?

Research has shown that the appropriate use of ICTs can catalyze the paradigmatic shift in both content and pedagogy that is at the heart of education reform in the 21st century.[19] If designed and implemented properly, ICT supported education can promote the acquisition of the knowledge and skills that will empower students for life-long learning.

When used appropriately, ICTs—especially computers and Internet technologies— enable new ways of teaching and learning rather than simply allow teachers and students to do what they have done before in a better way. These new ways of teaching and learning are underpinned by constructivist theories of learning and constitute a shift from a teacher-centered pedagogy—in its worst form characterized by memorization and rote learning—to one that is learner-centered. *(See Table 7.2 on next page for a comparison of a traditional pedagogy and an emerging pedagogy enabled by ICTs.)*

- ***Active learning:*** ICT-enhanced learning mobilizes tools for examination, calculation and analysis of information, thus providing a platform for student inquiry, analysis and construction of new information. Learners therefore learn as they do and, whenever appropriate, work on real-life problems in-depth, making learning less abstract and more relevant to the learner's life situation.

  In this way, and in contrast to memorization-based or rote learning, ICT-enhanced learning promotes increased learner engagement. ICT-enhanced learning is also 'just-in-time' learning in which learners can choose what to learn when they need to learn it.
- ***Collaborative learning:*** ICT-supported learning encourages interaction and cooperation among students, teachers, and experts regardless of where they are. Apart from modelling real-world interactions, ICT-supported learning provides learners the opportunity to work with people from different cultures, thereby helping to enhance learners' teaming and communicative skills as well as their global awareness. It models learning done throughout the learner's lifetime by expanding the learning space to include not just peers but also mentors and experts from different fields.
- **Creative Learning.** ICT-supported learning promotes the manipulation of existing information and the creation of real-world products rather than the regurgitation of received information.

Table 7.2 : Overview of Pedagogy in the Industrial versus the Information Society

Aspect	Less (traditional pedagogy)	More (emerging pedagogy for the information society)
Active	• Activities prescribed by teacher	• Activities determined by learners
	• Whole class instruction	• Small groups
	• Little variation in activities	• Many different activities
	• Pace determined by the programme	• Pace determined by learners
Collaborative	• Individual	• Working in teams
	• Homogeneous groups	• Heterogeneous groups
	• Everyone for him/herself	• Supporting each other
Creative	• Reproductive learning	• Productive learning
	• Apply known solutions to problems	• Find new solutions to problems
Integrative	• No link between theory and practice	• Integrating theory and practice
	• Separate subjects	• Relations between subjects
	• Discipline-based	• Thematic
	• Individual teachers	• Teams of teachers
Evaluative	• Teacher-directed	• Student-directed
	• Summative	• Diagnostic

Source: Thijs A, *et. al.*, Learning Through the Web Available Online http//www.decIdenet.nl/Publications/Web_Exed_Learning pdf/Accessed 31 May 2002.

- ***Integrative learning***. ICT-enhanced learning promotes a thematic, integrative approach to teaching and learning. This approach eliminates the artificial separation between the different disciplines and between theory and practice that characterizes the traditional classroom approach.

- **Evaluative learning.** ICT-enhanced learning is student-directed and diagnostic. Unlike static, text- or print-based educational technologies, ICT-enhanced learning recognizes that there are many different learning pathways and many different articulations of knowledge. ICTs allow learners to explore and discover rather than merely listen and remember.

THE USES OF ICTS IN EDUCATION

Education policymakers and planners must first of all be clear about what educational outcomes (as discussed above) are being targeted. These broad goals should guide the choice of technologies to be used and their modalities of use.

The potential of each technology varies according to how it is used. Haddad and Draxler identify at least five levels of technology use in education: presentation, demonstration, drill and practice, interaction, and collaboration.[20]

Each of the different ICTs—print, audio/video cassettes, radio and TV broadcasts, computers or the Internet—may be used for presentation and demonstration, the most basic of the five levels. Except for video technologies, drill and practice may likewise be performed using the whole range of technologies. On the other hand, networked computers and the Internet are the ICTs that enable interactive and collaborative learning best; their full potential as educational tools will remain unrealized if they are used merely for presentation or demonstration.

How Have Radio and TV Broadcasting Been Used in Education?

Radio and television have been used widely as educational tools since the 1920s and the 1950s, respectively. There are three general approaches to the use of radio and TV broadcasting in education:[21]

1. *direct class teaching,* where broadcast programming substitutes for teachers on a temporary basis;

2. *school broadcasting,* where broadcast programming provides complementary teaching and learning resources not otherwise available; and
3. *general educational programming over community,* national and international stations which provide general and informal educational opportunities.

The most notable and best documented example of the *direct class teaching* approach is Interactive Radio Instruction (IRI).This consists of "ready-made 20-30 minute direct teaching and learning exercises to the classroom on a daily basis. The radio lessons, developed around specific learning objectives at particular levels of maths, science, health and languages in national curricula, are intended to improve the quality of classroom teaching and to act as a regular, structured aid to poorly trained classroom teachers in under-resourced schools."[22] IRI projects have been implemented in Latin America and Africa. In Asia, IRI was first implemented in Thailand in 1980; Indonesia, Pakistan, Bangladesh and Nepal rolled out their own IRI projects in the 1990s.[23] What differentiates IRI from most other distance education programs is that its primary objective is to raise the quality of learning—and not merely to expand educational access—and it has had much success in both formal and non-formal settings.[24] Extensive research around the world has shown that many IRI projects have had a positive impact on learning outcomes and on educational equity. And with its economies of scale, it has proven to be a cost-effective strategy relative to other interventions.[25]

Mexico's *Telesecundaria* is another notable example of direct class teaching, this time using broadcast television. The programme was launched in Mexico in 1968 as a cost-effective strategy for expanding lower secondary schooling in small and remote communities.Perraton describes the programme thus:

Centrally produced television programmes are beamed via satellite throughout the country on a scheduled basis (8 am to 2 pm and 2 pm to 8 pm) to Telesecundaria schools, covering the same secondary curriculum as that offered in ordinary schools. Each hour focuses on a different subject area and typically follows the same routine—15 minutes of television, then book-led and teacher-led activities. Students are exposed to a variety of teachers on television but have one home teacher at the school for all disciplines in each grade.[26]

The design of the programme has undergone many changes through the years, shifting from a 'talking heads' approach to more interactive and dynamic programming that "link[s] the community to the programme around the teaching method. The strategy meant combining community issues into the programs, offering children an integrated education, involving the community at large in the organization and management of the school and stimulating students to carry out community activities."[27]

Assessments of Telesecundaria have been encouraging: drop out rates are slightly better than those of general secondary schools and significantly better than in technical schools.[28] In Asia, the 44 radio and TV universities in China (including the China Central Radio and Television University), Universitas Terbuka in Indonesia, and Indira Ghandi National Open University have made extensive use of radio and television, both for direct class teaching and for school broadcasting, to reach more of their respective large populations. For these institutions, broadcasts are often accompanied by printed materials and audio cassettes.

Japan's University of the Air was broadcasting 160 television and 160 radio courses in 2000. Each course consists of 15 45-minute lectures broadcast nationwide once a week for 15 weeks. Courses are aired over University-owned stations from 6 am to 12 noon. Students are also given supplemental print materials, face-to-face instruction, and online tutorials.[29]

Often deployed with print materials, cassettes and CD-ROMS, school broadcasting, like *direct class teaching*, is geared to national curricula and developed for a range of subject areas. But unlike direct class instruction, school broadcasting is not intended to substitute for the teacher but merely as an enrichment of traditional classroom instruction. School broadcasting is more flexible than

IRI since teachers decide how they will integrate the broadcast materials into their classes. Large broadcasting corporations that provide school broadcasts include the British Broadcasting Corporation Education Radio TV in the United Kingdom and the NHK Japanese Broadcasting Station. In developing countries, school broadcasts are often a result of a partnership between the Ministry of Education and the Ministry of Information.

General educational programming consists of a broad range of programme types—news programs, documentary programs, quiz shows, educational cartoons, etc.—that afford non-formal educational opportunities for all types of learners. In a sense, any radio or TV programming with informational and educational value can be considered under this type. Some notable examples that have a global reach are the United States-based television show *Sesame Street*, the all-information television channels *National Geographic* and *Discovery*, and the radio programme *Voice of America*. The *Farm Radio Forum*, which began in Canada in the 1940s and which has since served as a model for radio discussion programmes worldwide, is another example of non-formal educational programming.[30]

What is Teleconferencing and What Have Been Its Educational Uses?

Teleconferencing refers to "interactive electronic communication among people located at two or more different places."[31] There are four types of teleconferencing based on the nature and extent of interactivity and the sophistication of the technology: (1) audio conferencing; (2) audio-graphic conferencing, (3) videoconferencing; and (4) Web-based conferencing.

Audio conferencing involves the live (real-time) exchange of voice messages over a telephone network. When low-bandwidth text and still images such as graphs, diagrams or pictures can also be exchanged along with voice messages, then this type of conferencing is called audio graphic. Non-moving visuals are added using a computer keyboard or by drawing/writing on a graphics tablet or whiteboard. *Videoconferencing* allows the exchange not just of voice and graphics but also of moving images. Video-conferencing technology does not use telephone lines but either a satellite link or television network (broadcast/cable). *Web-based conferencing*, as the name implies, involves the transmission of text, and graphic, audio and visual media via the Internet; it requires the use of a computer with a browser and communication can be both synchronous and asynchronous.

Teleconferencing is used in both formal and non-formal learning contexts to facilitate teacher-learner and learner-learner discussions, as well as to access experts and other resource persons remotely. In open and distance learning, teleconferencing is a useful tool for providing direct instruction and learner support, minimizing learner isolation. For instance, an audio graphic teleconferencing network between Tianjin Medical University in China and four outlying Tianjin municipalities was piloted in 1999 as part of a multi-year collaboration between Tianjin Medical University and the University of Ottawa School of Nursing funded by the Canadian International Development Agency. The audio graphic teleconferencing network aims to provide continuing education and academic upgrading to nurses in parts of Tianjin municipality where access to nursing education has been extremely limited.[32] Other higher education institutions using teleconferencing in their online learning programmes include the Open University of the United Kingdom, Unitar (University Tun Abdul Ruzak) in Malaysia, Open University of Hong Kong, and Indira Gandhi National Open University.

Promoting Learner-centered Pedagogy Through Computers

Project CHILD (Computers Helping Instruction and Learning Development) is a computer-integrated instruction programme developed in 1988 by the University of Florida for grades K-5 (pre-school and primary school).The programme focuses on three subject areas—reading, writing and mathematics. Each Project CHILD classroom has a learning station with between three to six computers. Butzin describes a typical Project CHILD classroom scenario thus:

- A class period begins with the teacher conducting a whole group lesson—let's says an introduction to fractions. After about 10 minutes of direct instruction, the students fan out to their first assigned learning station. Each station will have an activity related to fractions. Some stations will focus on skill practice, while others will focus on concept development. The station activities encompass kinesthetic (hands-on) learning as well as auditory and visual modalities. The teacher assigns instructional software at each computer station to tie in with the lesson objectives.
- As student groups work at their stations, the teacher circulates to help, probe, assess, and encourage students as they work on their assigned tasks. When a student finishes an activity...[s/he] moves on [to the next station] as needed. At the end of the period, the teacher gathers the class together for reflection and discussion on the day's activities.
- Teachers form cross grade subject-specific clusters (K-2 or 3-5) and work with children over three years, the better to judge what software is appropriate for the subject and to allow students to learn at their own pace.

Teachers are also given one year training on integration and are provided with research-based materials for lesson planning and technology integration.

Over a decade's worth of research on Project CHILD students have shown that they have scored consistently higher on standardized tests than their counterparts in traditional classrooms, and that the positive effects of the programme have increased over time. Project CHILD students also exhibited better attitudes toward school and learning, and better discipline as well. Project CHILD has been recognized as an effective programme by the

U.S. Department of Education's National Diffusion Network and has received funding for nationwide expansion.

Source: Butzin, S.,"Project CHILD: A Decade of Success for Young Children". Available Online http://www.thejournal.com/magazine/vault/A2882.cfm Accessed 22 June 2002.

How Have Computers and the Internet Been Used for Teaching and Learning?

There are three general approaches to the instructional use of computers and the Internet, namely:

1. Learning about computers and the Internet, in which technological literacy is the end goal;
2. Learning with computers and the Internet, in which the technology facilitates learning across the curriculum; and
3. Learning through computers and the Internet, integrating technological skills development with curriculum applications.[33]

What Does It Mean to Learn About Computers and the Internet?

Learning about computers and the Internet focuses on developing technological literacy. It typically includes:

- Fundamentals: basic terms, concepts and operations
- Use of the keyboard and mouse
- Use of productivity tools such as word processing, spreadsheets, data base and graphics programs
- Use of research and collaboration tools such as search engines and email
- Basic skills in using programming and authoring applications such as Logo or HyperStudio
- Developing an awareness of the social impact of technological change.[34]

South Korean Universities Go Virtual

South Korea has one of the most advanced ICT infrastructures in the world—computer penetration is extensive, and broadband Internet access is one of the best globally. The pervasiveness of ICT use in South Korean society has spilled over to the higher educational system.

South Korea currently has 15 single-mode virtual universities that offer only ICT-based courses. Among these are the Korea Cyber University, the Korea Digital University, and the Open Cyber University. These universities specialize in lifelong learning and vocational education—a deliberate strategy to prevent unnecessary competition with more established campus-based universities—and have a combined projected enrolment of 17,200 in 2002. Courses offered cover a wide range of fields, including technology, management, law, languages, social sciences, education, and theology.

Online courses are also offered by over 100 of South Korea's dual-mode universities. Ewha Woman's University, for instance, offers Internet-based courses in language, e-learning, drug prevention, in-service teacher training, and Korean and Women's studies for local and foreign students as well as working adults.

The accelerated adoption of virtual education in South Korea was a result of deliberate planning by government.

It began in 1998 with the launch of the Virtual University Trial Project (VUTP).With 65 universities and five companies participating, the VUTP was designed to:

1. create a cost-effective virtual education system without diminishing quality;
2. develop and implement Web-based or other types of distance education courses;
3. identify appropriate policies and standards for running a virtual university; and
4. share experiences during the trial period.

Participating institutions experimented with various technologies: satellite broadcasting, videoconferencing, video-on-demand, intranets, and the Internet. Based on the VUTP experience, detailed criteria for establishing virtual universities in South Korea were added to the Lifelong Education Law.

Two years after the VUTP, however, policymakers and educators in South Korea continue to grapple with issues of quality management, capacity building, cost-savings, open access, and the appropriateness of the instructional model for adult learners.

Source: Jung, In Sung," Virtual Education at the Tertiary Level: The Experience of Korea". Available Online http://www.TechKnow Logia.org... Accessed 4 July 2002.

What About Learning with Computers and the Internet?

Learning with the technology means focussing on how the technology can be the means to learning ends across the curriculum. It includes:

- Presentation, demonstration, and the manipulation of data using productivity tools;
- Use of curriculum-specific applications types such as educational games, drill and practice, simulations, tutorials, virtual laboratories, visualizations and graphical representations of abstract concepts, musical composition, and expert systems;
- Use of information and resources on CD-ROM or online such as encyclopaedia, interactive maps and atlases, electronic journals and other references.[35]

Technological literacy is required for learning with technologies to be possible, implying a two-step process in which students learn about the technologies before they can actually use them to learn. However, there have been attempts to integrate the two approaches.

What Does Learning Through Computers and the Internet Mean?

Learning through computers and the Internet combines learning about them with learning with them. It involves learning the technological skills 'just-in-time' or when the learner needs to learn them as he or she engages in a curriculum-related activity. For example, secondary school students who must present a report on the impact on their community of an increase in the price of oil for an Economics class may start doing research online, using spreadsheet and database programs to help organize and analyze the data they have collected, as well using a word processing application to prepare their written report.

How Are Computers and the Internet Used in Distance Education?

Many higher educational institutions offering distance education courses have started to leverage the Internet to improve their programmer's reach and quality. The Virtual University of the Monterrey Institute of Technology in Mexico uses a combination of print, live and recorded broadcasts, and the Internet to deliver courses to students throughout Mexico and in several Latin American countries. Similarly, the African Virtual University, initiated in 1997 with funding support from the World Bank, uses satellite and Internet technologies to provide distance learning opportunities to individuals in various English-speaking and French-speaking countries throughout Africa.

At the University of the Philippines Open University, course materials are still predominantly printbased but online tutorials are becoming a convenient alternative to face-to-face tutorials especially for students unwilling or unable to go to UPOU's various physical learning centers. About 70-90 per cent of UPOU's degree courses offer online tutorials as an option, while in several of its non-degree courses tutorials are conducted only online.

But even in Korea, where infrastructure is among the best in the world, and government has put considerable financial and other resources behind an ambitious ICT-based re-tooling of its educational system, challenges to online education persist. *(See Box 7.1 on page 128)*

Internet- and Web-based initiatives have also been developed at the secondary education level. The Virtual High School is a result of efforts of a nationwide consortium of school districts in the United States to promote the development and sharing of Web-based courses. In Canada, Open School offers a wide range of courses and resources to grades K-12 teachers and students that meet the requirements of the British Columbia curriculum. Course delivery is done through a mix of broadcast and video, while some courses are delivered totally online.[36]

The biggest movers in e-Learning, however, are not found within academe but in the private sector. John Chambers, CEO of Cisco, famously predicted that e-learning would be the next big killer application, and corporations are moving aggressively to fulfill this prediction. Merrill Lynch estimates that the combined higher education and corporate e-Learning markets in the US will grow from $US2.3 billion in 2000 to US$18 billion in 2003, with corporate training accounting for almost two thirds of that growth.[37] Indeed, the number of corporate universities have grown from 400 to 1,800 over the last 13 years. Corporate universities are primarily in-house organizations in large multinational companies that make use of videoconferencing and the Internet for employee training.[38] If this rate of growth continues, the number of corporate universities will exceed the number of traditional universities by 2010.[39] A parallel development in business is the growth of a new breed of companies that offer online training services to small- and medium-sized enterprises.[40]

What is Telecollaboration?

Online learning involving students logging in to formal courses online is perhaps the most commonly thought of application of the Internet in education. However, it is by no means the only application. Web-based collaboration tools, such as email, listservs, message boards, real-time chat, and Web-based conferencing, connect learners to other learners, teachers, educators, scholars and researchers, scientists and artists, industry leaders and politicians—in short, to any individual with access to the Internet who can enrich the learning process.

The organized use of Web resources and collaboration tools for curriculum appropriate purposes is called telecollaboration. Judi Harris defines *telecollaboration* as "an educational endeavor that involves people in different locations using Internet tools and resources to work together. Much educational telecollaboration is curriculum-based, teacher-designed, and teacher-coordinated. Most use e-mail to help participants communicate with each other. Many telecollaborative activities and projects have Web sites to support them."[41] The best telecollaborative projects are those that are fully integrated into the curriculum and not just extra-curricular activities, those in which technology use enables activities that would not have been possible without it, and those that empower students to become active, collaborative, creative, integrative, and evaluative learners (*See Box 7.1 on page 128*).There are currently hundreds of telecollaborative projects being implemented worldwide and many more that have either been completed or are in development.

One example is the Voices of Youth[42] project developed by UNICEF. It encourages students to share their views on global issues, such as HIV/AIDS and child labour, with other youth and adults around the world through an electronic discussion forum. The Voices of Youth website also provides background information on the different discussion topics as well as resource materials to help teachers integrate the Voice of Youth discussions in their other classroom activities.

The International Telementor Program (ITP)[43] links students with mentor-experts through email and discussion forums. Founded in 1995 with support from Hewlett Packard, ITP provides project-based online mentoring support to 5th to 12th grade and university students, especially from at-risk communities. The ITP telementor typically meets online with the student at least once every two weeks to answer questions, discuss key issues, recommend useful resources, and comment on student output. The teacher's role, on the other hand, is to provide support to both student and telementor, monitor the telementoring process, and track the student's progress.

Perhaps the most widely cited telecollaborative project is the Global Learning and Observations to Benefit the Environment (GLOBE) Program.[44] GLOBE is a U.S. Government-sponsored programme launched in 1994 that links primary and secondary students and teachers from over 10,000 schools in more than 95 countries to the scientific research community. GLOBE gives students the opportunity to collaborate with scientists in conducting earth science research. Participating students periodically take measurements of the atmosphere, water, soils, and land cover at or near their schools, following strict protocols designed by GLOBE scientists. They then enter this data to a central Web-based database. The database may be accessed by scientists, researchers and the general public. GLOBE also provides teachers with guidelines and materials for structured learning activities that take off from the students' hands-on experience. Students can also go to the GLOBE website for visualizations of the data they and other students have collected.

ISSUES IN THE USE OF ICTS IN EDUCATION

Effectiveness, cost, equity, and sustainability are four broad intertwined issues which must be addressed when considering the overall impact of the use of ICTs in education.

Does ICT-enhanced Learning Really Work?

The educational effectiveness of ICTs depends on how they are used and for what purpose. And like any other educational tool or mode of educational delivery, ICTs do not work for everyone, everywhere in the same way.

Enhancing access: It is difficult to quantify the degree to which ICTs have helped expand access to basic education since most of the interventions for this purpose have been small-scale and under-reported. One exception is the television-based project Telesecundaria (discussed in a previous section), which in 1997-98 was serving over 750,000 junior secondary students in 12,000 centers in Mexico. In Asia and Africa, assessments of distance learning projects at the junior secondary level using a combination of print, taped, and broadcast technologies have been less conclusive, while at the primary level there is little evidence that ICT-based models have thrived.[45] In higher education and adult training, there is some evidence that educational opportunities are being opened to individuals and groups who are constrained from attending traditional universities. Each of the 11 so-called mega-universities, the biggest and most well-established open and distance institutions in the world (which include the Open University of the United Kingdom, the Indira Gandhi National Open University of India, the China TV University System, the Universitas Terbuka of Indonesia, and the University of South Africa, among others) has an annual enrollment of more than 100,000, and together they serve approximately 2.8 million. Compare that with the 14 million combined enrollment of the 3,500 colleges and universities in the United States.[46]

Raising quality: The impact of educational radio and television broadcasts on the quality of basic education remains an under-researched area, but what little research there is suggests that these interventions are as effective as traditional classroom instruction.[17] Of the many educational broadcast projects, the Interactive Radio Instruction project has been the most comprehensively analyzed. Findings provide strong evidence of the project's effectiveness in raising the quality of education as demonstrated by increased scores on standardized tests as well as improved attendance.[48]

In contrast, assessments of the use of computers, the Internet and related technologies for distance learning have been equivocal. Russell, in his comprehensive review of research, claims that there is 'non-significant difference' between the test scores of learners taking ICT-based distance learning courses and those receiving face-to-face instruction.[49] However, others claim that such generalizations are inconclusive, pointing out that the large number of articles on ICT-based distance learning does not include original experimental research or case studies.[50] Other critics argue that dropout rates are much higher when instruction is delivered at a distance via ICTs.

There have also been many studies that seem to support the claim that the use of computers enhances and amplifies existing curricula, as measured through standardized testing. Specifically, research shows that the use of computers as tutors, for drill and practice, and for instructional delivery, combined with traditional instruction, results in increases in learning in the traditional curriculum and basic skills areas, as well as higher test scores in some subjects compared to traditional instruction alone.

Students also learn more quickly, demonstrate greater retention, and are better motivated to learn when they work with computers.[51] But there are those who claim that these represent modest gains and, in any case, much of the research on which these claims are based are methodologically flawed. Research likewise suggests that the use of computers, the Internet, and related technologies, given adequate teacher training and support, can indeed facilitate the transformation of the learning environment into a learner-centered one. But these studies are criticized for being mostly exploratory and descriptive in nature and lacking in empirical rigor. There is as yet no strong evidence that this new learning environment fosters improved learning outcomes. What does exist are qualitative data based on observations and analysis of student and teacher perceptions that suggest a positive impact on learning.[52]

One of the most critical problems in trying to assess the effectiveness of computers and the Internet as transformational tools is that standardized tests cannot capture the kinds of benefits that are expected to be gained in a learner-centered environment. Moreover, since technology use is fully integrated into the larger learning system, it is very difficult to isolate the technology variable and determine whether any observed gains are due to technology use or to some other factor or combination of factors.

How Much Does It Cost?

Broadly speaking, educational television broadcasts and computer-based and online learning are more expensive than radio broadcasts.[53] There is disagreement, however, over whether television broadcasts are cheaper than computer-based and online learning.[54] That said, categorical assessments of cost-effectiveness are difficult to make because of lack of data, differences in programs, problems of generalization, and problems of quantification of educational outcomes and opportunity costs.[55]

Speaking specifically of computers and the Internet, Blurton argues that "[w]hen considering whether ICT is 'cost-effective' in educational settings, a definitive conclusion may not be possible for a variety of reasons. However, when considering the alternative of building more physical infrastructure, the cost savings to be realized from sharing resources, and the societal price of not providing access, ICT as a means of enabling teaching and learning appears to be an attractive and necessary alternative."[56]

A common mistake in estimating the cost of a particular ICT educational application is to focus too much on initial fixed costs—purchase of equipment, construction or retrofitting of physical facilities, initial materials production, and the like. But studies of the use of computers in classrooms, for example, show that installation of hardware and retrofitting of physical facilities account for only between 40 per cent to 60 per cent of the full cost of using the computers over their lifetime, or its *total cost of ownership*.[57] In fact, while at first glance it may seem that the initial purchase of hardware and software is the costliest part of the process, the bulk of the total cost of ownership is spread out over time, with annual maintenance and support costs (known as variable or recurrent costs) constituting between 30 per cent to 50 per cent of the total cost of hardware and software. The cost of professional development, another variable cost, also accumulates over time.

For computer-based approaches the total cost of ownership therefore includes:

Fixed Costs

- Retrofitting of physical facilities
- Hardware and networking
- Software
- Upgrades and replacement (in about five years)

Variable or Recurrent Costs

- Professional development
- Connectivity, including Internet access and telephone time
- Maintenance and support, including utilities and supplies

In order to determine cost efficiencies, fixed costs must be distinguished from variable costs, and the balance between the two understood. If the fixed costs of a technology project are high and its variable costs are low, then there will be cost advantages to scaling up. This is the case with general educational radio and television broadcasting. Programs such as Sesame Street and Discovery are more cost-efficient the larger their audience since the high cost of production is distributed over a larger viewer base while no staff expenditures are made for learner support.

On the other hand, the case of Telesecundaria in Mexico demonstrates that the impact of higher variable costs related to learner support may be offset if the scale of the project is sufficiently large to the point where per student costs compare favorably with those of traditional schools. Similarly, with the Interactive Radio Instruction project annual cost per student is estimated to fall from US$8.25 with 100,000 students to US$3.12 with 1,000,000.[58] Obviously, these economies of scale may be achieved only in countries with large populations. Open and distance learning institutions have also achieved cost-effectiveness through economies of scale. Per student costs of the 11 mega-universities range from only 5 per cent to 50 per cent of the average of the traditional universities in their respective countries.[59]

The introduction of computers represents additional costs for schools but without short-term cost advantages. Data on cost of computer use per student in both primary and secondary schools in fact suggest cost-ineffectiveness. In Chile, for example, cost per primary school student is between US$22 and US$83, with expenditures for computer use requiring 10 per cent to 37 per cent of the national primary school budget.[60] In the U.S., computer investments accounted for 1.3 per cent of total expenditure on schools, with annual cost per student at US$70.[61]

Perraton and Creed suggest that these levels of cost support the argument against putting computers in every classroom, particularly in primary schools where there are no strong curricular arguments for investment in computers. In secondary schools, spending money on computers may be justified by the curriculum but this will come with significant increases in total school expenditure.[62]

Another dimension of cost is location, or who will pay for what. In projects that involve computers connected to the Internet, either the school or student or both bear the variable costs related to operations such as maintenance, Internet service charges, and telephone line charges. In contrast, with radio programming the learner has to pay only for a radio and a set of batteries.

Is There Equity of Access to ICTs in Education?

Given the wide disparities in access to ICTs between rich and poor countries and between different groups within countries, there are serious concerns that the use of ICTs in education will widen existing divisions drawn along economic, social, cultural, geographic, and gender lines. Ideally, one wishes for equal opportunity to participate. But access for different actors—both as users and producers—is weighted by their resources. Hence, initial differences are often reproduced, reinforced, and even magnified....A formidable challenge, therefore, continues to face planners of international education: how to define the problem and provide assistance for development.[63]

The introduction of ICTs in education, when done without careful deliberation, can result in the further marginalization of those who are already underserved and/or disadvantaged. For example, women have less access to ICTs and fewer opportunities for ICT-related training compared to men because of illiteracy and lack of education, lack of time, lack of mobility, and poverty.[64] Boys are more likely than girls to have access to computers in school and at home. Not surprisingly, boys tend to enjoy working with computers more than girls.[65] As the American Association of University Women reports, "Girls have narrowed some significant gender gaps, but technology is now the new 'boys' club' in our nation's public schools. While boys programme and problem solve with computers, girls use computers for word processing..."[66]

In an evaluation of its programme in four African countries, Worldlinks,[67] an organization that promotes project-based, international telecollaboration activities among secondary school teachers and students from developing countries, it was found that despite efforts to make the programme gender neutral, gender inequalities in access persist in Uganda and Ghana. Furthermore, while girls benefited more from the programme in terms of improved academic performance and communication skills, boys were able to hone their technological skills more. A complex of economic, organizational, and socio-cultural factors account for these differences: "High student-to-computer ratios and first come first serve policies do not favour girls (typically heavily outnumbered by boys at the secondary level), girls have earlier curfew hours and domestic chore responsibilities which limit their access time, and local patriarchal beliefs tend to allow boys to dominate the computer lab environment."[68] Measures proposed to address this gender bias include encouraging schools to develop 'fair use' policies in computer labs, conducting gender sensitivity sessions, and advocating for reducing the after-school duties of girls to give them more time to use the computer lab.[69] Girls also need to have female role models to inspire them to participate in technology-related activities.[70]

Providing access to ICTs is only one facet of efforts to address equity issues. Equal attention must be paid to ensuring that the technology is actually being used by the target learners and in ways that truly serve their needs. An ICT-supported educational programme that illustrates this wholistic approach is the *Enlace Quiché*: Bilingual Education in Guatemala Through Teacher Training programme.[71] The programme seeks to establish and maintain bilingual education technology centers for educators, students, teachers, parents, and community members in Quiché and neighboring areas. The technical teams for each centre are composed of three students, two teachers, and the centre administrator, with at least one female student and one female teacher. Another objective of *Enlace Quiché* is the creation of multimedia bilingual educational materials that are anchored on the Mayan culture and that reflect a constructivist approach to learning. As the project website notes, this "demonstrate[s] that the technology can be used to know, to conserve, to disclose and to value local knowledge." The project thus illustrates a model for bridging the digital divide arising from the monopoly in Internet content provision by Western and English-speaking groups and from uneven capacities to make purposeful, relevant and critical use of digital resources (see section on language and content below).

Another example of a wholistic approach to ICT integration in education is a radio instruction project in Mongolia called the Gobi Women's Project. It seeks to provide literacy and numeracy instruction built around lessons of interest to around 15,000 nomadic women, and to create income opportunities for them. Among the programme topics are livestock rearing techniques; family care (family planning, health, nutrition and hygiene); income generation using locally available raw materials; and basic business skills for a new market economy.[72]

Are ICT-enhanced Educational Projects Sustainable?

One aspect of development programmes that is often neglected is sustainability. The long history of development aid has shown that too many projects and programmes start with a bang but all too soon fade out with a whimper, to be quickly forgotten. This is true for many ICT-based educational projects as well. In many instances, these projects are initiated by third party donors—such as international aid agencies or corporations—and not enough attention is paid to establishing a mechanism by which the educational institution or community involved can pursue the project on its own or in partnership with other stakeholders after the initiating donor exits. But cost and financing are not the only barriers to sustainability. According to Cisler, the sustainability of ICT-enabled programmes has four components: social, political, technological, and economic.[73]

Economic sustainability refers to the ability of a school and community to finance an ICT-enabled programme over the long term. Cost-effectiveness is key, as technology investments typically run high and in many cases divert funds from other equally pressing needs. Planners should look to the total cost of ownership *(see preceding discussion on cost)* and build lucrative partnerships with the community to be able to defray all expenses over the long term. The need to develop multiple channels of financing through community participation ties economic sustainability closely to social and political sustainability.

Social sustainability is a function of community involvement. The school does not exist in a vacuum, and for an ICT-enabled project to succeed the buy-in of parents, political leaders, business leaders and other stakeholders is essential. Innovation can happen only when all those who will be affected by it, whether directly or indirectly, know exactly why such an innovation is being introduced, what the implications are on their lives, and what part they can play in ensuring its success. ICT-enabled programmes must ultimately serve the needs of the community. Thus community-wide consultation and mobilization are processes critical to sustainability. In short, a sense of ownership for the project must be developed among all stakeholders for sustainability to be achieved.

Political sustainability refers to issues of policy and leadership. One of the biggest threats to ICTenabled projects is resistance to change. If, for instance, teachers refuse to use ICTs in their classrooms, then use of ICTs can hardly take off, much less be sustained over the long term. Because of the innovative nature of ICT-enabled projects, leaders must have a keen understanding of the innovation process, identify the corresponding requirements for successful adoption, and harmonize plans and actions accordingly.

Technological sustainability involves choosing technology that will be effective over the long term. In a rapidly changing technology environment, this becomes a particularly tricky issue as planners must contend with the threat of technological obsolescence. At the same time, there is the tendency to acquire only the latest technologies (which is understandable in part because these are the models which vendors are likely to push aggressively) Generally, however, planners should go with tried and tested systems; stability issues plague many of the latest technologies. Again, the rule of thumb is to let the learning objectives drive the technology choice and not vice versa—the latest technologies may not be the most appropriate tools for achieving the desired educational goals. When making technology decisions, planners should also factor in not just costs but also the availability of spare parts and technical support.

KEY CHALLENGES IN INTEGRATING ICTS IN EDUCATION

Although valuable lessons may be learned from best practices around the world, there is no one formula for determining the optimal level of ICT integration in the educational system. Significant challenges that policymakers and planners, educators, education administrators, and other stakeholders need to consider include educational policy and planning, infrastructure, language and content, capacity building, and financing.

What are the Implications of ICT-enhanced Education for Educational Policy and Planning?

Attempts to enhance and reform education through ICTs require clear and specific objectives, guidelines and time-bound targets, the mobilization of required resources, and the political commitment at all levels to see the initiative through. Some essential elements of planning for ICT are listed below:

(*a*) A rigorous analysis of the present state of the educational system. ICT-based interventions must take into account current institutional practices and arrangements. Specifically, drivers and barriers to ICT use need to be identified, including those related to curriculum and pedagogy, infrastructure, capacity-building, language and content, and financing.

(*b*) The specification of educational goals at different education and training levels as well as the different modalities of use of ICTs that can best is employed in pursuit of these goals. This requires of the policymaker an understanding of the potentials of different ICTs when applied in different contexts for different purposes, and an awareness of priority education needs and financial and human resource capacity and constraints within the country or locality, as well as best practices around the world and how these practices can be adapted for specific country requirements.

(*c*) The identification of stakeholders and the harmonizing of efforts across different interest groups.

(*d*) The piloting of the chosen ICT-based model. Even the best designed models or those that have already been proven to work in other contexts need to be tested on a small scale. Such pilots are essential to identify, and correct, potential glitches in instructional design, implement ability, effectiveness, and the like.

(*e*) The specification of existing sources of financing and the development of strategies for generating financial resources to support ICT use over the long term.

What are the Infrastructure-related Challenges in ICT-Enhanced Education?

A country's educational technology infrastructure sits on top of the national telecommunications and information infrastructure. Before any ICT-based programme is launched, policymakers and planners must carefully consider the following:

- In the first place, are appropriate rooms or buildings available to house the technology? In countries where there are many old school buildings, extensive retrofitting to ensure proper electrical wiring, heating/cooling and ventilation, and safety and security would be needed.
- Another basic requirement is the availability of electricity and telephony. In developing countries large areas are still without a reliable supply of electricity and the nearest telephones are miles away. Experience in some countries in Africa point to wireless technologies (such as VSAT or Very Small Aperture Terminal) as possible levers for leapfrogging.[74] Although this is currently an extremely costly approach, other developing countries with very poor telecommunications infrastructure should study this option.
- Policymakers should also look at the ubiquity of different types of ICT in the country in general, and in the educational system (at all levels) in particular. For instance, a basic requirement for computer-based or online learning is access to computers in schools, communities, and households, as well as affordable Internet service.

In general, ICT use in education should follow use in society, not lead it. Education programs that use cutting-edge technologies rarely achieve long term success: It is cheaper, and easier, to introduce a form of technology into education, and keep it working, where education is riding on the back of large-scale developments by governments or the private sector. Television works for education when it follows rather than precedes television for entertainment; computers in schools can be maintained once commercial and private use has expanded to the point where there is an established service industry.[75]

What are the Challenges with Respect to Capacity-Building?

Various competencies must be developed throughout the educational system for ICT integration to be successful.

Teachers: Teacher professional development should have five foci: 1. skills with particular applications; 2. integration into existing curricula; 3. curricular changes related to the use of IT (including changes in instructional design); 4. changes in teacher role; and 5. underpinning educational theories.[76] Ideally, these should be addressed in pre-service teacher training and built on and enhanced in-service. In some countries, like Singapore, Malaysia, and the United Kingdom, teaching accreditation requirements include training in ICT use. ICTs are swiftly evolving technologies, however, and so even the most ICT fluent teachers need to continuously upgrade their skills and keep abreast of the latest developments and best practices.

Will ICTs Replace the Teacher?

The answer is a resounding NO! In fact, with the introduction of ICTs in the classroom, the teacher's role in the learning process becomes even more critical. What can and should change is the kind of role that the teacher plays. The role of students, in turn, also expands. And since ICTs can open up the classroom to the outside world, the community can also play a new role in the classroom.

As learning shifts from the 'teacher-centered model' to a 'learner-centered model', the teacher becomes less the sole voice of authority and more the facilitator, mentor and coach—from 'sage on stage' to 'guide on the side'. The teacher's primary task becomes to teach the students how to ask questions and pose problems, formulate hypotheses, locate information and then critically assess the information found in relation to the problems posed.

And since ICT-enhanced learning is a new experience even for the teachers, the teachers become co-learners and discover new things along with their students.[77] Additionally, it is not uncommon to see students in an ICT-enabled classroom assume both formal and informal roles as teachers of their peers and younger students, sometimes even of their own teachers. Teachers and students from different schools, subject-matter experts, parents, community and business leaders, politicians, and other interested parties also become involved in the learning process—as resource persons, critics, mentors, and cheerleaders. They also comprise a public, and hopefully critical, audience for students' work published on the Web or through other media.[78]

Yet many teachers are reluctant to use ICTs, especially computers and the Internet. Hannafin and Savenye identify some of the reasons for this reluctance: poor software design, skepticism about the effectiveness of computers in improving learning outcomes, lack of administrative support, increased time and effort needed to learn the technology and how to use it for teaching, and the fear of losing their authority in the classroom as it becomes more learner-centered.[79] These are all issues that must be addressed by both pre-service teacher education and in-service teacher professional development programs if schools and other educational institutions are to fully exploit the potential of computers and the Internet as educational tools.

At the in-service level, ICT teacher professional development (TPD) should be long-term, teacher-directed, and as flexible as possible. For many under-qualified, overworked, and underpaid teachers in developing countries, effective adoption of ICTs hinges on being given continuous opportunities to learn what they need to learn based on their specific circumstances and experience, when they have the time to learn it. Institutionalized incentives and support for teachers to pursue ICT TPD are also critical. This may take the form of promotions for teachers who innovate with (as opposed to merely using) ICTs in the classroom, or simply making sure that teachers have adequate access to technology after training.

While the first focus—skills with particular applications—is self-evident, the four other foci are of equal, if not ultimately greater, importance. Research on the use of ICTs in different educational settings over the years invariably identify as a barrier to success the inability of teachers to understand why they should use ICTs and how exactly they can use ICTs to help them teach better.

Unfortunately,most teacher professional development in ICTs are heavy on 'teaching the tools' and light on 'using the tools to teach.'

Box 7.1. WorLD: Teacher Professional Development as the Cornerstone of Educational ICT Use

The World Links for Development (WorLD) Program began in Uganda in 1997 under the auspices of the WorLD Bank Institute. Its goal was to help government to bring the benefits of the Internet and the WorLD Wide Web to the country's secondary schools. The WorLD Programme has three components. Connectivity, Training and Monitoring and Evaluation. While many international and local organizations have focused on providing technology to schools. WorLD has, over the years, built an impressive repulation as one of the world's leading providers of professional development services to teachers school administrators and policymakers in developing countries around the world. WorLD's Professional Development Programme for Teachers, which is delivered primarily face-to-face by international and local trainors, with follow-ups online, are in five phases :

Phase 0	:	Computer Literacy.
Objective	:	To introduce the fundamentals of computer technology and help participants acquire basic computer literacy knowledge and skills.
Phase 1	:	Introduction to the Internet for Teaching and Learning.
Objective	:	Introduce fundamental concepts, technologies and skills necessary for introducing networked technology and the Internet to teaching and learning: initiate dicussion of new possibiliities, generate basic email projects.
Phase 3	:	Introduction to Telecollaborative Learning Projects.
Objective	:	Introduction to educational telecollaboration–from activity structures to the creation, design, implementation and dissemination of original projects.
Phase 4	:	Curriculum and Technology Integration.
Objective	:	Develop Skills and understanding of how to create, incorporate and facilitate innovative classroom practices that integrate networked technology and curricula.

Phase 4 : Innovations: Pedagogy, Technology and Professional Development.

Objective : Develop skills and understanding of how to evaluate and diffuse innovative classroom practices while addressisng social and ethical concerns.

WorLD has also developed training models for policymakers on educational ICT management and on telecenters. WorLD is currently active in over 20 countries in Africa, Latin America and South Asia. It is set to roll out its programmes in Southeast Asia—in Cambodia, Laos, Vietnam, Indonesia and the Philippines—in 2003.

Source: WorLD.Programme Profile, 2001.

Teacher anxiety over being replaced by technology or losing their authority in the classroom as the learning process becomes more learner-centered—an acknowledged barrier to ICT adoption—can be alleviated only if teachers have a keen understanding and appreciation of their changing role.

Education administrator: Leadership plays a key role in ICT integration in education. Many teacher- or student-initiated ICT projects have been undermined by lack of support from above. For ICT integration programs to be effective and sustainable, administrators themselves must be competent in the use of the technology, and they must have a broad understanding of the technical, curricular, administrative, financial, and social dimensions of ICT use in education.

Technical support specialists. Whether provided by in school staff or external service providers, or both, technical support specialists are essential to the continued viability of ICT use in a given school. While the technical support requirements of an institution depend ultimately on what and how technology is deployed and used, general competencies that are required would be in the installation, operation, and maintenance of technical equipment (including software), network administration, and network security. Without on-site technical support, much time and money may be lost due to technical breakdowns.

In the Philippines, for example, one of the major obstacles to optimizing computer use in high schools has been the lack of timely technical support. In some extreme cases involving schools in remote areas, disabled computers take months to be repaired since no technician is available in the immediate vicinity and so the computers have to be sent to the nearest city hundreds of kilometers away.[80]

Content developers: Content development is a critical area that is too often overlooked. The bulk of existing ICT-based educational material is likely to be in English (see section on language and content below) or of little relevance to education in developing countries (especially at the primary and secondary levels). There is a need to develop original educational content (e.g., radio programmes, interactive multimedia learning materials on CD-ROM or DVD, Web-based courses, etc.), adapt existing content, and convert print-based content to digital media. These are tasks for which content development specialists such as instructional designers, scriptwriters, audio and video production specialists, programmers, multimedia course authors, and web-developers are needed. Like technical support specialists, content developers are highly skilled professionals and are not, with the exception of instructional designers, historically employed by primary and secondary schools. Many universities with distance education programmes, and those who otherwise make use of ICTs, have dedicated technical support and content development units.

What Challenges Need to be Addressed in the Areas of Language and Content?

English is the dominant language of the Internet. An estimated[80] per cent of online content is in English.[81] A large proportion of the educational software produced in the world market is in English. For developing countries in the Asia-Pacific where English language proficiency is not high, especially outside metropolitan areas, this represents a serious barrier to maximizing the educational benefits of the World Wide Web.

Even in countries where English is a second language (such as Singapore, Malaysia, the Philippines, and India) it is imperative that teaching and learning materials that match national curriculum requirements and have locally meaningful content, preferably in the local languages, be developed. (*See Box 7.2*). This would ensure that the Web is a genuinely multicultural space and that peoples of different cultures have an equal stake and voice in the global communities of learning and practice online. Particularly vulnerable to exclusion of this sort are isolated, rural populations, cultural minorities, and women in general. Thus attention must be paid to their special needs.

One encouraging trend has been the emergence of national and regional school networks, or School Nets, that facilitate the sharing of content and information—curriculum guides, teaching and learning resources, telecollaborative project registries, school and teacher directories, training curricula and materials, research and policy papers, technology management guides, and start-up toolkits, among others. Countries like Australia, France, Finland, Japan, Canada, Thailand, Ghana, South Africa, and Zimbabwe, to name a few, all have national SchoolNets.The Enlaces programme in Latin America has linked schools from Spanish-speaking countries like Chile, Paraguay, Costa Rica, Colombia, and Peru. In Southeast Asia, efforts are currently underway to pilot School Nets in the Philippines, Indonesia, Cambodia, Laos, Myanmar and Vietnam, and to link these to existing national School Nets to create a region-wide ASEAN School Net.

In Web-based learning, technical standardization of content has also become a pressing issue. Standardization allows different applications to share content and learning systems. Specifications in content, structure, and test formats are proposed so that interoperability may exist between different management systems, resulting in some cost-efficiencies. Standards must be general enough to support all kinds of learning systems and content. Worth mentioning are initiatives conducted by the Instructional Management System (IMS), the Advanced Distributed Learning / Shareable Courseware Object Reference Model (ADL/SCORM) initiative, the Aviation Industry Computer Based Training Committee

(AICC), and the European ARIADNE project, since some of the standards they have proposed are already being widely applied.

The ease by which Web-based educational content can be stored, transmitted, duplicated, and modified has also raised concerns about the protection of intellectual property rights. For instance, is intellectual, property rights violated when lectures broadcast over the television or on the Web incorporate pre-existing materials, or when students record educational broadcast on tape for later viewing? While schools and universities may already have agreements that expressly authorize the use of certain materials for classroom purposes, these agreements may not be broad enough to accommodate telecommunications transmission, videotape recording, or the distribution of course-related materials beyond the classroom setting.[82]

The United Nations International World Intellectual Property Organization is leading international efforts in setting global standards for the protection of intellectual property rights that would not at the same time unduly curtail the accessing and sharing of information. For teachers and students, each of whom are potential publishers of multimedia materials that incorporate the works of others, information and training about the ethical use of intellectual property should be an important component of ICT-based programs.[83]

What are the Challenges Related to Financing the Cost of ICT Use?

One of the greatest challenges in ICT use in education is balancing educational goals with economic realities. ICTs in education programs require large capital investments and developing countries need to be prudent in making decisions about what models of ICT use will be introduced and to be conscious of maintaining economies of scale. Ultimately it is an issue of whether the value added of ICT use offsets the cost, relative to the cost of alternatives. Put another way, is ICT-based learning the most effective strategy for achieving the desired educational goals, and if so what is the modality and scale of implementation that can be supported given existing financial, human and other resources?

Content is King: Lessons from Thailand

Three years after its inception in 1995, School Net Thailand, a joint project of the National Electronics and Computer Technology Center (NECTEC), the Telephone Organization of Thailand, the Communications Authority of Thailand, and the Ministry of Education, found itself facing a challenge it had not entirely expected. Having built a network infrastructure for education in Thailand that connected 152 local secondary schools to the Internet, it discovered that schools hardly used the Internet as a tool for teaching and learning. It soon became apparent that the lack of quality educational online resources in the local language, Thai, was discouraging Internet use among teachers and students. SchoolNetThailand thus had to expand what had largely been a 'universal access' programme to include content development—complemented by training—in the Thai language.

In September 1998, School Net Thailand commissioned Kasetstart University and the Institute for the Promotion of Teaching Science and Technology to create Thai language websites on secondary school-level Mathematics, Physics, Chemistry, Biology, Engineering, the Environment, and Computer Science. Collectively called the 'Digital Library', these websites were launched a little over a year later. School Net Thailand also developed an easy-to-use web authoring application called the 'Digital Library Tool Kit' that allowed teachers to create Web-based lessons in Thai. Teachers and students were also given instruction on web page development. By May 2001, the Digital Library already contained 1,113 lessons, created mostly by classroom teachers. Complementing the 'Digital Library' project was the production of multimedia professional development materials called 'Thai Teacher 2000' which included a printed manual, a video tape, and a CD-ROM. School Net Thailand's content development efforts also benefited from a national documentation project spearheaded by the Office of the National Cultural Commission called 'Thai Cultural Information System.' This programme was intended to, among others, collect information on Thai culture and disseminate this information through CD-ROMs and the Internet.

At present, School Net Thailand boasts of approximately 4,000 schools in its network, with over 900 of these with their own web pages in Thai. It expects to extend Internet service provision to the estimated 34,000 schools nationwide in the coming years and to continue to lead in local content development in Thailand.

Source: NECTEC. (July 2002). ICT for Poverty Reduction: Examples of Programmes/Projects in Thailand, pp. 6-13.

The ease by which Web-based educational content can be stored, transmitted, duplicated, and modified has also raised concerns about the protection of intellectual property rights. For instance, is intellectual, property rights violated when lectures broadcast over the television or on the Web incorporate pre-existing materials, or when students record educational broadcast on tape for later viewing?

While schools and universities may already have agreements that expressly authorize the use of certain materials for classroom purposes, these agreements may not be broad enough to accommodate telecommunications transmission, videotape recording, or the distribution of course-related materials beyond the classroom setting.[82]

The United Nations International World Intellectual Property Organization is leading international efforts in setting global standards for the protection of intellectual property rights that would not at the same time unduly curtail the accessing and sharing of information. For teachers and students, each of whom are potential publishers of multimedia materials that incorporate the works of others, information and training about the ethical use of intellectual property should be an important component of ICT-based programmes.[83]

What are the Challenges Related to Financing the Cost of ICT Use?

One of the greatest challenges in ICT use in education is balancing educational goals with economic realities. ICTs in education programmes require large capital investments and developing countries need to be prudent in making decisions about what models of ICT use will be introduced and to be conscious of maintaining economies of scale. Ultimately it is an issue of whether the value added of ICT use offsets the cost, relative to the cost of alternatives. Put another way, is ICT-based learning the most effective strategy for achieving the desired educational goals, and if so what is the modality and scale of implementation that can be supported given existing financial, human and other resources?

Whyte suggests the following potential sources of money and resources for ICT use programmes:

1. Grants
2. Public subsidies
3. Private donations, fund-raising events
4. In-kind support (e.g., equipment, volunteers)
5. Community support (e.g. rent-free building)
6. Membership fees
7. Revenues earned from core business:
    - Connectivity (phone, fax, Internet, web pages)
    - Direct computer access to users
    - Office services (photocopying, scanning, audio-visual aids
8. Revenues earned from ancillary activities:
    - Business services (word-processing, spreadsheets, budget preparation, printing, reception services)
    - Educational services (distant education, training courses)
    - Community services (meeting rooms, social events, local information, remittances from migrant workers)
    - Telework and consulting

- Specialized activities (telemedicine)
- Sales (stationary, stamps, refreshments, etc.)[84]

Private sector-public sector partnerships to either pilot or fast track ICT-based projects are a strategy that has gained currency among Ministries of Education in developing countries. These partnerships take many forms, including private sector grants with government counterpart contributions, donations of equipment and education-related content by corporations to state-run schools, and the provision of technical assistance for planning, management, and strengthening human resources at the grassroots level. Multilateral organizations and international aid agencies have also driven many of the most significant ICT in education efforts in the developing world.

But the financial litmus test of ICT-based programmes is survival after donor money has run out. Many ICTbased education programs funded by aid agencies or by corporations could not be sustained because government failed to step in with the necessary financing; nor were the local communities in a position to generate the resources needed to continue these programs. This was the case with some of the Interactive Radio Instruction projects initiated by USAID. Therefore, a two-fold strategy is key: government support and local community mobilization.

Will ICT Use Be the Silver Bullet That Will Rid a Developing Country of All of Its Educational Problems?

If there is one truism that has emerged in the relatively brief history of ICT use in education, it is this: It is not the technology but how you use it! Put another way: "How you use technology is more important than if you use it at all…[and] unless our thinking about schooling changes along with the continuing expansion of [ICTs] in the classroom then our technology investment will fail to live up to its potential."[85]

Technology then should not drive education; rather, educational goals and needs, and careful economics, must drive technology use. Only in this way can educational institutions in developing countries effectively and equitably address the key needs of the population, to help the population as a whole respond to new challenges and opportunities created by an increasingly global economy. ICTs, therefore, cannot by themselves resolve educational problems in the developing world, as such problems are rooted in well entrenched issues of poverty, social inequality, and uneven development. What ICTs as educational tools can do, if they are used prudently, is enable developing countries to expand access to and raise the quality of education. Prudence requires careful consideration of the interacting issues that underpin ICT use in the school—policy and politics, infrastructure development, human capacity, language and content, culture, equity, cost, and not least, curriculum and pedagogy.

Box 7.2. Coke is IT : Corporate Social Responsibility in the Information Age

The Coca-Cola Company's ICT in Education partnerships with governments, multilateral organizations, non-govermental organications and educators in the Asia Pacific began in 1997 with the establishment of the first Coca-Cola Learning Center in Ho ChiMinh City, Vietnam Coca-Cola has since expanded the approach to four other countries in the region—the Philippines, China, Malaysia and Australia—bringing e-Larning opportunities and resources to tens of thousands of young people and their communities.

Vietnam

Partners	:	Coca-Cola Ministry of Education & Training and the National Youth Union
Funding	:	US$375,000
Programme Highlights	:	Forty Learning Centres set up in secondary schools and youth centres in 33 cities and provinces. Programme provides Internet access, educational software and textbooks to students and teachers.

Australia

Partners	:	Coca-Cola, Microsoft Australia and the Inspire Foundation
Funding	:	US$184,000

Programme Highlights.	:	Launched in March 2001. Ten "Beanbag Net Centres" for disadvantaged youth in urban areas Programme provides Internet access. IT training and dedicated local websites for young people.
Philippines		
Partners	:	Coca-Cola, Department of Education and the Foundation for IT Education and Development
Funding	:	US$450,000
Programme Highlights	:	Launched in April 2001. Fifteen 'Edventure" centres setup in secondary schools in six provinces. Programme provides Internet access and technology-based educational resources and ttraining for teachers, students, and school administrators. Centres are used for teaching ICT skills, Math, Science, Languages and History. Centres are open for community use.
China		
Partners	:	Coca-Cola and the China Youth Development Foundation
Funding	:	US$400,000
Programme Highlights	:	Launched in May 2001. Twenty "e-Learning for Life" centres set up in remote Project Hope primary schools across the country. Programme provides Internet access, educational content and training on ICT skills for teachers, students and local communities. Centres are used for the teaching of Math, Chinese, English and History.
Malaysia		
Partners	:	Coca-Cola Ministry of Education and the United Nations Development Programme
Funding	:	US$360,000
Programme Highlights	:	Launched in March 2002. Six ICT 'hubs' set up in secondary schocls in peri-urban and rural areas. Programme provides wireless Internet access, educational software and training for students and teachers. Participating schools are integrating computer lab-based training into existing curricula. ICT 'hubs' also double as community access centers.

"This is an existing 21st century extension of our support of youth education in Asia. We know that finding sustainable ways to bridge the digital divide is a real priority for many countries in Asia and were committed to doing our part in helping. We do this through partnerships that take their care from loal leaders and experts. We've been focussed on building local community ownership into each of these initiatives from the get-go. This helps ensure sustainability over time," explains Coca-Cola Asia's Stuart Hawkins.

It remains to be seen whether each of these country-level projects will indeed have a future without Coca-Cola. Prospects for the Malaysia project seem good—built into the programme design is the transfer of ownership and operational responsibility to the Malaysian government after one year. In the Philippines the 15 school-based e-Learning centres are making some inroads towards sustainability through community involvement and capacity building although prospects for institutionalization remain unclear.

Source: Coca-Cola Asia. Project Fast Shoeets, August 2002.

REFERENCES

1. US Department of Labour (1999), *Futurework—Trends and Challenges for Work in the 21st Century. Quoted in EnGauge*, "21st Century Skills," North Central Regional Educational Laboratory; available from http://www.ncrel.org/engauge/skills/21skills.htm; accessed 31 May, 2002.
2. For a Convincing Argument for the Need to Transform Notions of 'Schooling' in Light of Technology Driven Social Change See Thornburg, David (2000),"Technology in K-12 Education: Envisioning a New Future"; available from http://www.air-dc.org/forum/abthornburg.htm; accessed 3 July, 2002.
3. International Labour Organization, "Learning and Training for Work in the Knowledge Society;" available from *http://www.llo.org/public/English/employment/skills/* recommit/report; accessed 31 May, 2002, p. 5.
4. Blurton, C., "New Directions of ICT-Use in Education". Available online *http://www.unesco.org/education/* educprog/lwf/dl/edict.pdf; accessed 7 August, 2002.
5. See for example Cuban, L. (1986), *Teachers and Machines: The Classroom Use of Technology Since 1920* (New York: Teachers College Press).

6. Potashnik,M.and J.Capper,"Distance Education: Growth and Diversity;" available from *http://www.worldbank.* org/fandd/english/pdfs/0398/0110398.pdf; accessed 14 August, 2002.
7. See Taghioff, Daniel (April 2001),"Seeds of Consensus—The Potential Role for Information and Communication Technologies in Development: Empowerment, Appropriateness and Measuring If Needs Really Get Met;" available from *http://www.btinternet.com/~daniel.taghioff/index.html*; accessed 14 August, 2002.
8. *http://www.open.ac.uk*
9. *http://www.ignou.ac.in*
10. The Commonwealth of Learning," An Introduction to Open and Distance Learning"; available from http://www.col.org/ODLIntro/introODL.htm; accessed 14 August, 2002.
11. Quoted in Founts, Jeffrey T. (February 2000),"Research on Computers and Education: Past, Present and Future"; available from *http://www.gatesfoundation.org/nr/dpwnloads/* ed/evaluation/Computer_Research_Summary.pdf; accessed 30 October, 2002, p. 11.

12 World Bank (1998), *The World Development Report 1998/99. Quoted in Blurton, C., New Directions of ICT-Use in Education.*

13. EnGauge. North Central Regional Educational Laboratory; available from http://www.ncrel.org/engauge/skills/21skills.htm; accessed 31 May, 2002.
14. Haddad,Wadi D. and Jurich, Sonia (2002),"ICT for Education: Potential and Potency", in Haddad,W. & Drexler, A. (eds),*Technologies for Education: Potentials, Parameters, and Prospects* (Washington DC: Academy for Educational Development and Paris: UNESCO), pp. 34-37.
15. Jung, I.," Issues and Challenges of Providing Online In-service Teacher Training: Korea's Experience"; available from http://www.irrodl.org/content/v2.1/jung.pdf; accessed 4 August, 2002.
16. Carnoy,Martin, *et al.* (June 2, 2001),"Distance Education in China: A Discussion of the History, Challenges and Implications for China in the 21st Century"; available from http://ldt.stanford.edu/~yokonaga/portfolio/ed236x/China.jjy.htm; accessed 4 August, 2002.
17. http://www.ignou.ac.in. See also Asian Development Bank (1997), *Distance Education for Primary School Teachers: Papers and Proceedings of the Regional Seminar on Distance Education* (Manila: Asian Development Bank).

18. International Center for Distance Learning,"Universitas Terbuka/ Indonesian Open Learning University"; available from *http://www-icdl.open.ac.uk/* instResult.ihtml?inst_id=5777&p=1; accessed 14 August 2002.
19. See for example Bransford, J. (ed.) (1999), H*ow People Learn: Brain, Mind, Experience, and School* (Washington,DC: National Research Council).
20. Haddad,Wadi D. & Alexandra Drexler (2002),"The Dynamics of Technologies for Education", in Haddad,W. & Drexler, A. (eds.) *Technologies for Education: Potentials, Parameters, and Prospects* (Washington DC: Academy for Educational Development and Paris: UNESCO), p. 9.
21. Perraton, H. and C. Creed," Applying New Technologies and Cost-Effective Delivery Systems in Basic Education"; available from *http://unesdoc.unesco.org/images/* 0012/001234/12348 2e.pdf; accessed 31 May 2002. Perraton and Creed use the term "General Children's Programming" to refer to the broad target audience of basic education. Although their discussion is limited to this level of education, the broadcasting approaches they identify may also be applied to other educational levels.
22. *Ibid.,* p. 13.
23. TechnKnowLogia,"Are You Talkin' to Me?: Interactive Radio Instruction"; available from *http://www.techknowlogia.org/ TKL_active_pages2/CurrentArticles/main.asp?IssueNumber= 2&File* Type=PDF&ArticleID=46; accessed 29 May 2002.
24. Bosch, A., "Interactive Radio Instruction for Mathematics: Applications and Adaptations from Around the World"; available from *http://www.techknowlogia.org/TKL_active_pages2/Current Articles/main.asp?FileType=HTML&Arti* cleID=255; accessed 15 August 2002, p. 45.
25. *Ibid.,* pp. 48-49.
26. Perraton, H. and C. Creed," Applying New Technologies..."
27. UNESCO,"Telesecundaria,Mexico"; available from http:// www.unesco.org/education/educprog/lwf/protfolio/ abstract8.htm; accessed 15 August 2002, p. 2.
28. Perraton, H. and C. Creed," Applying New Technologies...
29. Iwanaga, M.,"The Present and the Future of Multimedia in Japan's Open Learning"; available from http://www.ouhk.edu.hk/ cridal/gdenel/Technology/technology.html; accessed 11 January 2002.

30. Nwaerondu, N.G. and G.Thompson,"The Use of Educational Radio in Developing Countries: Lessons from the Past" ; available from http://www.clrec.org/nwaeronduthompson; accessed 3 May, 2002, pp. 2-3.
31. Rao,V. Rama,"Audio Teleconferencing—A Technological Prescription for Interactive Learing"; available from http://www.clrec.org/rama; accessed 14 August, 2002.
32. Edwards, N."Development and Integration of Web-based Technology in Distance Education for Nurses in China: A Pilot Study"; available from *http://www.clerc.org/* edwardsn; accessed 9 June, 2002.
33. Richmond, Ron. *Integration of Technology in the Classroom: An Instructional Perspective.* SSTA Research Centre Report #97-02; available from *http://www.ssta.sk.ca/* research/technology/97-02.htm#BIBLIOGRAPHY; accessed 30 October, 2002.
34. *Ibid.*
35. *Ibid.*
36. Dirr, R.,"The Development of New Organizational Arrangements in Virtual Learning", in *The Changing Faces of Virtual Education*; available from http://www.col.org/virtualed/virtual2pdfs/Virtual2_complete.pdf; accessed 7 August 2002
37. Moe, M. and H. Blodget,"The Knowledge Web". Cited in A.Bates,"The Continuing Evolution of ICT Capacity: Implications for Education", in Glen M.Farrell (ed.), *The Changing Faces of Virtual Education; available from http://www.col.org/virtualed/virtual2pdfs/Virtual2_complete.pdf*; accessed 7 August 2002.
38. Bates, A." The Continuing Evolution of ICT Capacity: Implications for Education", in Glen M.Farrell (ed.), *The Changing Faces of Virtual Education*; available from http://www.col.org/virtualed/virtual2pdfs/Virtual2_complete.pdf; accessed 7 August 2002.
39. Web-based Education Commission," The Power of the Internet for Learning"; available from
40. http://www.ed.gov/offices/AC/WBEC/Final Report/WBECReport.pdf; accessed 12 April 2002.
41. *Ibid.*
42. Harris, Judi, "First Steps in Telecollaboration"; available from http://ccwf.cc.utexas.edu/~jbharris/Virtual-Architecture/Articles/First-Steps.pdf; accessed 6 March, 2002, p. 1.
43. *http://www.unicef.org/voy*

44. *http://www.telementor.org*
45. *http://www.globe.org*
46. Perraton, H. and C. Creed," Applying New Technologies...", p. 38-39. Potashnik, M. and J. Capper. (1998)."Distance Education...", p. 42, 44.
47. Hannafin, R.D., & Savenye, S. (1993).Technology in the Classroom...
48. Perraton, H. and C. Creed, "Applying New Technologies...", pp. 38-39.
49. Russel,T.L (1999). *The No Significant Difference Phenomenon* (5th ed.). Raleigh NC: North Carolina State University.
50. Merisotis, Jamie P. and Ronald A. Phipps (1999,May/June),What's the Difference? Outcomes of Distance *vs.* Traditional Classroom-based Learning, in *Change*, pp. 13-17.
51. Fouts, J. (February 2002). Research on Computers and Education: Past, Present and Future; available from *http://www.gatesfoundation.org/nr/downloads/ed/evaluation/* Computer_Research_Summary.pdf; accessed 30 October 2002.
52. *Ibid.*
53. Blurton, C.,"New Directions of ICT-Use in Education", p. 21.
54. See for example, Blurton, C.,"New Directions of ICT-Use in Education" and Perraton, H. and C. Creed, "Applying New Technologies..."
55. Blurton, C., "New Directions of ICT-Use in Education", p. 20.
56. *Ibid.*, p. 24.
57. Consortium for School Networking," Taking TCO to the Classroom: A School Administrator's Guide to Planning for the Total Cost of New Technology"; available from http://ctap.fooo.k12.ca.us/clap/dhs3.4/tco2olacs.pdf; accessed 3 February 2002, p. 10.
58. Adkins,D. (1999), "Cost and Finance," in Dock, A. and Helwig, J. (eds.), *Interactive Radio Instruction: Impact, Sustainability, and Future Directions* (Washington DC:World Bank Human Development Network Education Group, Education and Technology Team/USAID Advancing Basic Education and Literacy Project, Education Development Center). Cited in Perraton, H. and C. Creed, "Applying New Technologies...," p. 40.
59. Potashnik, M. and J. Capper. (1998). "Distance Education...", p. 44.

60. Perraton, H. and C. Creed, "Applying New Technologies...," pp. 40-41.

61. Orivel, F. (2000), "Finance, Costs and Economics", in J.Bradley and C.Yates (eds.), *Basic Education at a Distance: World Review of Distance Education and Learning,* Vol. 2 (London: Routledge).

62. *Ibid.,* p. 41.

63. Hernes,G. (2002), "Emerging Trends in ICT and Challenges to Educational Planning," in Haddad,W. and A. Drexler (eds.), *Technologies for Education: Potentials, Parameters, and Prospects* (Washington DC: Academy for Educational Development and Paris: UNESCO), p. 25.

64. Tandon,N. (November 1998), "Distance Education in the Commonwealth Countries of Asia," Appendix to Commonwealth of Learning, *Barriers to Information and Communication Technologies Encountered by Women: Summary Report*; available from http://www.col.org/wdd/BarriersICT_Asia_Report.pdf; accessed 14 September 2002, p. 44.

65. Mark, J. "Beyond Equal Access: Gender Equity in Learning with Computers"; available from http://www.edc.org/WomensEquity/pubs/digests/digest-beyond.html; accessed 23 October 2002.

66. AAUW Education Foundation (14 October 1998), "Technology Gender Gap Develops While Gaps in Math and Science Narrow, AAUW Foundation Report Shows" [Press Release]; available from http://www.auuw.org/2000/ggpr.html.Quoted in Blurton, C., "New Directions of ICT-Use in Education", p. 44.

67. http://www.world-links.org

68. Gadio, C.M. (November 2001),"Exploring the Gender Impact of the World Links Programme: Summary of the Findings of an Independent Study Conducted in Four African Countries"; available from *http://www.world-links.org/english/assets/* gender_study_summary.pdf; accessed 6 December 2002, p. 1.

69. *Ibid.,* p. 2.

70. Haddad,W. and S. Jurich (2002). "ICT for Education: Potential and Potency", p. 52.

71. *http://www.enlacequiche.org.gt/english/vision.htm*

72. "The Gobi Women's Project of Mongolia: Portfolio"; available from*http://www.unesco.org/education/* educprog/lwf/doc/portfolio/case1.htm; accessed 16 January 2003.

73. S. Cisler,"Planning for Sustainability: How to Keep Your ICT Project Running"; available from http://www2.ctcnet.org/ctc/Cisler/sustain.doc; accessed 4 August, 2002.
74. Hawkins, R., "Ten Lessons for ICT and Education in the Developing World"; available from http://www.cid.harvard.edu/cr/pdf/gitrr2002_ch04.pdf; accessed 7 August 2002, p. 40.
75. Perraton, H. and C. Creed, "Applying New Technologies...", p. 41.
76. MacDougall, A. and D. Squires (1997), "A Framework for Reviewing Teacher Professional Development Programmes in Information Technology". Cited in Blurton, C.,"New Directions of ICT-Use in Education", p. 29.
77. World Links for Development. Phase II: Telecollaborative Learning Projects. Training Manual, June 2001,
78. *Ibid.*
79. Hannafin, R.D., and S. Savenye. (1993), "Technology in the Classroom: The Teacher's New Role and Resistance to It, in *Educational Technology*, 33 (6), 26-31.
80. Tinio,V. (2002), "Survey of ICT Utilization in Philippine Public High Schools: Preliminary Findings" [Unpublished Manuscript].
81. Anzalone, Stephen, "ICTs to Support Learning in Classrooms in SEAMEO Countries: At What Costs?". Paper prepared for SEAMEO conf. In Bangkok, March 26-9, 2001.
82. Salomon, K., "A Primer on Distance Learning and Intellectual Property Issues"; available from http://www.teletrain.com/copyrigh.htm#3.student%20Waivers; accessed 4 August 2002, p. 5.
83. Blurton, C., "New Directions of ICT-Use in Education", p. 35.
84. Whyte, A., "Assessing Community Telecentres. Guidelines for Researchers". cited in S. Cisler, "Planning for Sustainability..."
85. Thornburg, D., "Technology In K-12 Education...", p. 1.

For Further Reading

1. Bates, A.W. 2000. *Managing Technological Change: Strategies for University and College Leaders.* San Francisco: Jossey Bass.
2. Brown, J.S. and P.Duguid. 2000. *The Social Life of Information.* Boston MA:Harvard Business School Press.
3. Carlson, S. and C. T. Gadio. 2002. "Teacher Professional Development in the Use of Technology", in Haddad, W. and A.

Drexler (eds). *Technologies for Education: Potentials, Parameters, and Prospects.* Washington DC: Academy for Educational Development and Paris: UNESCO.

4. Cuban, L. 2002. *Oversold and Underused: Computers in the Classroom.* Cambridge MA: Harvard University Press.
5. Daniel, J. 1996. *Mega Universities and Knowledge Media: Technology Strategies for Higher Education.* London: Kogan Page.
6. Haddad,W. 1994. *The Dynamics of Education Policymaking: Case Studies of Burkina Faso, Jordan, Peru, and Thailand.* EDI Development Policy Case Series, Analytical Case Studies No. 10.Washington DC:The World Bank.
7. Steffe, L. P. and J.Gale.1995. *Constructivism in Education.* Hillsdale, NJ: Lawrence Erlbaum.
8. Rusten, E. and H. Hudson. 2002. "Infrastructure: Hardware, Networking, Software, and Connectivity", in Haddad, W. and A. Drexler (eds). *Technologies for Education: Potentials, Parameters, and Prospects.* Washington DC: Academy for Educational Development and Paris: UNESCO.

CHAPTER

Productivity Gains
Importance of ICTs

Australia's growth performance since the early 1990s has been remarkable. For nine years, annual growth averaged just under four per cent—a performance not seen since the 1960s and early 1970s. Strong growth even persisted in the midst of the 1997 Asian financial crisis and the 2001 global downturn.

A surge in productivity growth has underpinned Australia's good performance. After showing its weakest rate in the 1980s, Australia's productivity growth accelerated to record highs in the 1990s. The rate of growth in labour productivity from 1993-94 to 1999-2000 was 3.0 per cent a year (up from a previous average from the early 1980s of 1.7 per cent a year) and the rate of multifactor productivity (MFP) growth was 1.8 per cent a year (up from 0.7 per cent a year).

The 1990s productivity surge was also strong by international standards. Australia was one of three countries to show strong productivity acceleration in the 1990s (OECD, 2001a). It was a period, unlike the post-war 'golden age', when there was no worldwide productivity boom. Australia's rate of productivity growth out clipped the OECD average for the first time and out pointed the resurgent US rate.

Australia's surge started around 1993, or possibly earlier, although an uplift in underlying productivity growth prior to 1993 is difficult to disentangle from the effects of recovery from the 1990-91 recession (Parham, 1999, 2002a). In any case, Australia's surge predated the US productivity acceleration from 1995, which has been linked to an information and communication technology (ICT) boom.

The timing, strength and largely isolated nature of Australia's productivity surge point to the likelihood of some peculiarly Australian explanations. However, there is no single factor. Some credit should be given to deft macroeconomic policy settings, especially in the face of the Asian financial crisis. Education levels in the workforce have also risen markedly over the past two decades (Dowrick, 2002).

However, there is general agreement that microeconomic policy reforms have played a central role in Australia's productivity surge (see, for example, Productivity Commission, 1999; Bean, 2000; Dowrick, 2000; Forsyth, 2000; OECD, 2001b). Policy reforms, which have been introduced progressively since the mid-1980s, have included: deregulation of access to finance; marked reductions in barriers to trade and foreign direct investment; commercialisation (and some privatisation) of government business enterprises, which have controlled large parts of economic infrastructure; strengthening domestic competition; and increasing labour market flexibility.

Reforms have fostered productivity growth through three main avenues:

- sharpening incentives to be more productive, chiefly by strengthening competition;
- opening the economy to trade, investment and technologies developed overseas; and
- providing greater flexibility (for example, less regulatory restriction, more flexible labour markets) to adjust production processes and firm organisation to improve productivity.

The tendency to link Australia's productivity surge to policy reforms and not to an ICT boom has reinforced a view in some quarters that Australia has not accessed 'new economy' gains. Furthermore, the US evidence has been read to suggest that ICT production is needed to tap 'new economy' productivity gains. According to this view, the lack of a sizeable ICT production industry in Australia has been seen as a preventive barrier to ongoing higher productivity growth.

This chapter examines the issue of whether Australia has accessed 'new economy' productivity gains associated with ICTs. The US experience is used as a benchmark to determine upper bounds on the productivity gains that can attributed to ICT production and use. This chapter also draws out policy and statistical implications.

The Role of ICTs in Australia's Productivity Surge

This section reports on a conventional productivity growth accounting exercise, updated from Parham, Roberts and Sun (2001), which investigates the importance of ICTs in Australia's productivity surge.

The Nature of the Links Between ICTs and Productivity Gains

Computers, telecommunication systems and the Internet have brought revolutionary changes to businesses, consumers, education, health, entertainment and many other aspects of life. A defining characteristic is that the costs of storing, accessing and exchanging information have been greatly reduced. In so doing, ICTs have reduced the costs of coordination, communications and information processing. But, increasingly, they have also facilitated changes in what businesses do and how they do it.

A particular analytical interest has centered on the links between ICTs and productivity growth. Many studies of these links have employed a growth accounting framework, based on national accounts approaches to productivity estimation. This framework provides three avenues for ICTs to influence labour productivity:

- Increases in capital deepening. Labour productivity can rise as a result of higher capital use per unit of labour, as firms invest in more ICTs. Many analysts have noted this mechanism accords no special qualities to ICTs. As they have become cheaper, firms have substituted ICTs for labour and other forms of capital—as could happen for many other inputs.

- Productivity gains in ICT production. Producers' ability to manufacture much more powerful ICT equipment, with little increase in inputs, generates substantial MFP gains. If the gains are of sufficient magnitude and production is on sufficient scale, they can show up as contributions to aggregate MFP growth and labour productivity.
- Productivity gains in ICT-using industries. This is the most controversial source of ICT-related productivity gains. It requires that use of ICTs generates MFP gains. On the one hand, 'new economy' enthusiasts have pointed to MFP gains from such sources as increasing returns from ICT use and spillovers from network economies. On the other hand, sceptics have either denied or found little evidence to support the existence of MFP gains from use.

On the last point, there is, perhaps, some middle ground. For example, US Federal Reserve Board Chairman, Alan Greenspan, pointed to gains that he believes come from greater and cheaper access to information — greater certainty, through the availability of real-time information about customers' demands and the location of inventories and materials flowing through complex production systems, which leads to less wastage from extra production, inventories and staff; more efficient and compressed distribution processes; the development of financial instruments to manage risks; and lower search and transactions costs in business-to-business transactions (Greenspan, 2000a, 2000b).

Australia is an Advanced ICT User, Not Producer

The measurement of ICTs has an important bearing on the source and extent of estimated productivity gains associated with ICTs. The measurement of the volume of ICTs produced affects estimates of output and productivity growth in ICT production. The measurement of the volume of ICT investment affects estimates of growth in capital inputs and therefore the productivity residual in ICT-using industries.

In keeping with modern practice, the Australian Bureau of Statistics (ABS) uses hedonic (or constant-quality) price deflators to estimate real volumes of ICTs produced and purchased. Hedonic prices take into account changes in a number of characteristics of ICTs - processing speed, memory capacity and so on.

The quality-constant prices of ICT characteristics have declined markedly. This stems from the fact that while there have been rapid technological advances (especially in the capacity of microprocessors), there has been relatively little movement in the nominal prices of equipment.

Hedonic prices have not been specifically generated for ICTs in Australia. The ABS uses the US price deflator for hardware, adjusted for exchange rate movements and a time lag, and a Canadian price deflator for software. The US and Australian deflators are shown in Figure 8.1.

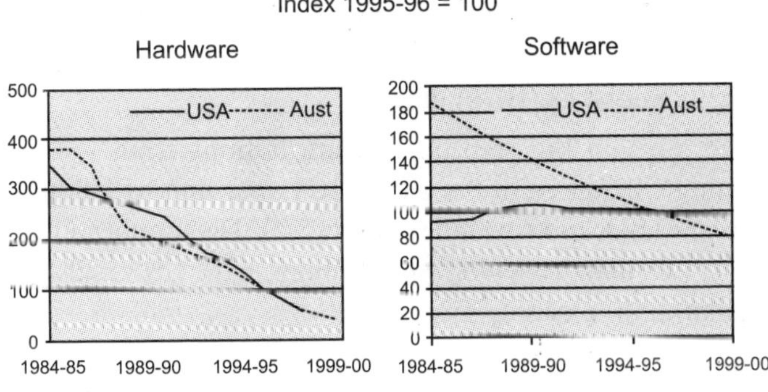

Source: Unpublished ABS data and BLS data.

Fig. 8.1: ICT Hardware and Software Price Indexes, USA and Australia

Investment in ICTs became a sizeable proportion of total investment in Australia from the mid-1980s. Since then, the growth of investment has been very strong, especially in the 1990s, when investment in hardware grew by 35 per cent a year and software investment grew by 20 per cent a year in real terms.

Australia became a high user by international standards, ranking fourth in 1999 among OECD countries in expenditure on ICTs as a proportion of GDP. Australia's rate of expenditure at 8.7 per cent of GDP came in ahead of the US rate at 8.0 per cent (OECD, 2001c).

In contrast, Australia ranks at the very low end of OECD countries in terms of size of its ICT equipment production industries. Australia imports most of its ICT equipment requirements.

ICT Contributions to Productivity Growth — The USA and Australia Compared

The contributions of ICTs to Australia's productivity growth are now assessed and compared with the US experience. Comparison with the USA helps to sort out the sources of Australia's productivity gains.

There have been a number of US studies of ICT contributions to productivity growth (for example, Oliner and Sichel, 2000; Jorgenson and Stiroh, 2000; and Gordon, 2000). For brevity, however, this chapter focuses on comparisons with the USA based on Bureau of Labour Statistics (BLS) data.

There was a big step up in contributions from ICT capital deepening (increases in the use of ICTs per unit of labour) from 1995 in the USA and Australia (Figure 8.2). The timing and strength of the ICT capital deepening contributions in the USA and Australia are remarkably close.

Most studies of the USA have compared productivity growth and ICT contributions before and after this 1995 takeoff. But 1995 was a trough year in US labour productivity, at a point below trend. Estimates from 1995 to the end of the 1990s are from a trough to a peak and therefore overstate the underlying rate of labour productivity growth. The ABS method of estimating productivity growth over productivity cycles—from productivity peak to productivity peak—is one way of measuring underlying rates of growth. Adopting this method puts the prime focus on accelerations in underlying rates of productivity growth, rather than on the ICT takeoff and its effects.

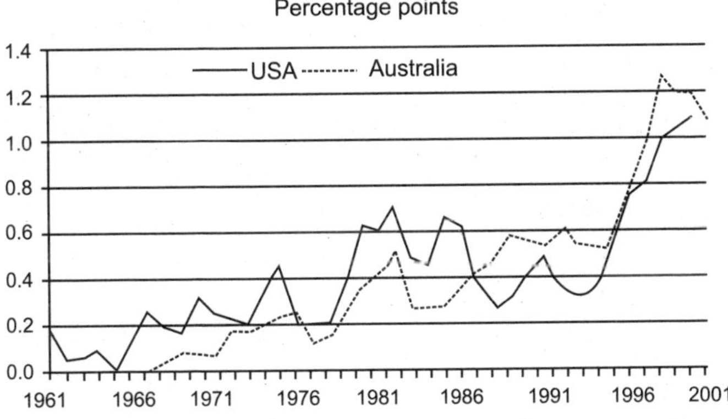

Source: Productivity Commission estimates based on unpublished ABS data and BLS data.

Fig. 8.2 : Contributions of ICT Capital Deepening to Labour Productivity Growth in the USA and Australia, 1961 to 2001

The 1990s peak-to-peak cycle for the USA is from 1992 to 2000 and for Australia from 1993-94 to 1999-2000. Contributions to the labour productivity accelerations in the 1990s cycle (compared with the previous cycle) in both countries are presented in table 8.1.

There are several similarities in the US and Australian results:

- ICTs have made strong capital deepening contributions to acceleration in productivity in both countries. The contribution is of a similar order of magnitude (around 0.3 to 0.4 of a percentage point) in both cases.
- However, much or all of the increased use of ICTs (per hour worked) in the 1990s has been offset by slower growth in the use of other forms of capital (per hour worked). There has been little or no increase in the overall rate of capital deepening in either country, especially in Australia (Table

8.1). This contrasts with most other studies of the USA, which have found that ICTs have contributed to a marked increase in the rate of substitution of capital for labour.

Table 8.1 : Contributions to Labour Productivity Accelerations in the 1990s Cycle in the USA and Australia

(Per cent per year)

	USA[a]	Australia[b]
Labour productivity growth	0.5	1.0
Capital deepening	0.2	–0.1
–ICT capital	0.3	0.4
–Other capital	–0.2	–0.5
MFP contribution[c]	0.3	1.1

Notes: [a]Growth in 1992 to 2000 loss growth in 1986 to 1992
[b]Growth in 1993-94 to 1999-00 less growth in 1988-89 to 1993-94
[c]MFP growth for the USA includes the contribution to labour productivity growth from labour quality

Source: Updated from Parham, Roberts and Sun (2001).

- Faster MFP growth accounts for most of the 1990s labour productivity accelerations in both countries, and entirely so in Australia.

The main difference between the US and Australian results lie in the strength of the productivity accelerations. The acceleration in underlying labour productivity growth in Australia, at one percentage point, is twice that in the USA. With similar capital deepening contributions, the chief explanation for the difference lies in the much stronger MFP acceleration in Australia (1.1 percentage point) than in the USA (0.3 of a percentage point).

The stronger productivity acceleration in Australia suggests that Australian firms benefited from one or both of two factors: bigger gains from the use of ICTs and more gains from non-ICT factors.

The first possibility is unlikely. It seems reasonable to assume, consistent with the US leadership in productivity and ICTs that the

US estimates establish the upper limit on productivity gains that can be associated specifically with ICT production and use. The more likely explanation is that Australian industries have had more scope to improve from a lower base and have caught up on at least some of the superior US levels (Parham, 2002a, 2000b). This catch-up is not specifically related to ICTs.

While the US estimates set the upper limit on ICT-related gains, some of the 0.3 of a percentage point MFP acceleration must be attributed to production of ICTs. Studies, such as Oliner and Sichel (2000), have attributed around 0.3 of a percentage point of aggregate MFP growth to ICT production, although the acceleration was calculated pre- and post-1995. The acceleration over productivity cycles would be less—perhaps half.

This leaves a contribution of perhaps 1 or 2 tenths of a percentage point from ICT use to the acceleration in underlying aggregate MFP growth in the USA. Even if the more favourable pre-and post-1995 figures are used, the most that can be attributed to ICT use is 0.3 of a percentage point (Parham, 2002a).

Applying these US benchmarks to the Australian case suggests that non-ICT factors have contributed the bulk (0.8 of a percentage point or more) to the acceleration in Australia's productivity growth. This part of the acceleration can be attributed largely to international catch-up and microeconomic policy reforms (Parham, 2002a). Creating a more competitive, open and flexible environment has encouraged and enabled Australian business to move toward established best practice. The remaining gains (up to 0.3 of a percentage point) would represent ICT-related gains associated with new products and new dimensions of best practice.

An Industry Perspective

While the evidence suggests that the aggregate MFP gains to date from ICT use are significant, but not spectacular, there is evidence of strong links in certain industries. Several studies of the USA have found evidence of productivity acceleration in the 1990s in Wholesale trade; Retail trade; Finance, insurance and real estate (especially in financial intermediation); and Business services. These industries have also been characterised as intensive users of ICTs (Stiroh, 2001; Nordhaus, 2001; Centre for the Study of Living Standards, 2000; Council Of Economic Advisors, 2001; Pilat and Lee, 2001).

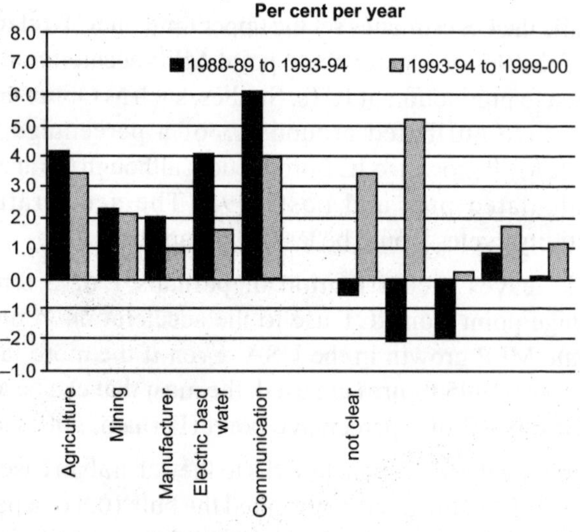

Source: PC estimates based on unpublished ABS data.

Fig. 8.3 : Industry MFP growth over the last two productivity cycles in Australia, 1988-89 to 1993-94 and 1993-94 to 1999-2000

A similar set of industries emerged in the 1990s as major contributors to Australia's productivity surge. Figure 8.3 presents MFP growth rates in industry sectors over the past two productivity cycles. In the first cycle (1988-89 to 1993-94), the relatively strong productivity growth in the 'traditional' contributors to aggregate productivity growth—Agriculture, Mining, and Manufacturing—is evident. These traditional sectors were joined in the 1980s and early 1990s by two other strong performers—Communication services and Electricity, gas and water. Their improved performance stemmed from major reform-induced efficiencies in government enterprises, which have dominated production in these two sectors, as well as technological advances in some activities. While productivity growth remained relatively strong in all five industry sectors in the 1990s cycle (except for Manufacturing), they all experienced a deceleration compared with the previous cycle. On these estimates, none made a contribution to the productivity surge from 1993-94. A new set of service industries made the positive contribution. The stand-out performer was Wholesale trade, suggesting that there have been major changes in traditional wholesaling activities of receiving and storing goods and disbursing them through resale to businesses. Other service industries—for example, Construction and Finance and insurance—also increased their rate of productivity growth.

There is no strong, positive relationship between ICT use and MFP across all Australian industries. There is a strong (above-average) positive relationship between increased ICT use and MFP acceleration in Finance and insurance and a weaker relationship in Wholesale trade. While the ICT link appears largely confined to these sectors, they are major parts of the economy, accounting for 6.6 per cent and 4.7 per cent respectively of Australia's GDP in 2000-01.

The lack of systematic relationship across all industries undoubtedly reflects the fact that ICT use is not the only factor affecting industry MFP growth. It also signals that the productivity gains from ICT use appear—for the moment at least— concentrated in distribution and financial intermediation. (There may also be ICT-productivity links at the firm level in other industries that, because of inter-firm differences in these and other factors, do not translate as readily into industry or aggregate trends—see Brynjolfsson and Hitt, 2000). The lack of a relationship across all industries also tends to support the view that the gains to date cannot be attributed to network economies, which could be expected to be more widespread.

The relationships between ICT use and productivity growth are complex. ICTs are often viewed as general-purpose technologies that require time to bring to their full potential and that provide a platform for other innovations in products and processes (see, for example, Brynjolfsson and Hitt, 2000; and Bresnahan, Brynjolfsson and Hitt, 2002).

The Australian evidence supports the view that it is the changes in products and processes that generate the productivity gains. The Finance and insurance industry has been restructured to operate much more through ICTs (for example, ATMs, Internet and phone banking) than through traditional face-to-face contacts. Many new products (for example, financial derivatives) are now on offer.

An earlier study by Productivity Commission staff (Johnston *et al*., 2000) also found that ICTs played a part in the restructuring of wholesaling activities. Wholesalers were able to use bar-code and scanning technology and inventory management systems as part of the process of transforming wholesaling from a storage-based to a fast flow-through operation that reduces storage and handling.

But, importantly, reforms were acting as the underlying drivers and facilitators of productivity gains and ICTs were just one component of change. It was not so much that wholesaling became much more ICT intensive or that new 'breakthrough' technologies became available. It was more that the competitive incentives to be productive became stronger and that new flexibilities became open to businesses to use ICTs as part of a more general process of restructuring and transformation.

For example, the motor vehicle industry was looking for efficiencies all along the 'value chain', including in distribution, to meet the increased competition from cheaper imports entering under lower border protection. Another contributor in some areas was the reform of industrial relations processes that allowed greater labour flexibility through the introduction of split shifts and reduced the rigidity of job demarcations.

Policy Implications

A major implication of the evidence in this and related Productivity Commission papers is that, from a productivity and policy perspective, a prime focus on ICTs and the 'new economy' is somewhat misplaced. There are three potential pitfalls:

- too much attention on ICT production as a source of productivity growth;
- insufficient attention on the factors that drive ICT use; and
- insufficient attention on other factors that are potentially the source of greater productivity gains.

On the first point, there have been calls for policy action to foster the development of ICT production in order to access 'new economy' productivity gains. However, the Australian (and the US) experience clearly demonstrates that there are also productivity gains associated with ICT use. ICT production is not necessary to access productivity gains. The US estimates suggest there have been roughly equal productivity gains at the aggregate level from ICT production and use. If anything, the gains from use may well accelerate further in the future. Further product and process innovation is possible and larger and more widespread network effects (associated, for example, with e-commerce) may start to show up.

It also needs to be remembered that the scope for productivity gains in production in the USA does not translate as readily to other countries as does the productivity gains from use. The US production gains come from a very large scale of operations and a degree of technological leadership that cannot be readily established in other countries. Aside from some niche areas (particularly in software), ICT production requires not only large scale operation but also sales in highly competitive international markets. This makes it tough going for a relatively small economy like Australia's.

Other advantages also come from focusing on use. By being open to imports of ICTs, Australia has been able to gain quickly from advances in ICT manufacture and has been able to capture a sizeable terms of trade gain from the rapidly declining international prices in ICTs. The Treasury (2002) stated that ICT prices have fallen in domestic currency terms by 9.5 per cent a year and raised the terms of trade by 0.3 per cent a year between 1985 and 2001. Since 1995, ICT prices have fallen by nearly 15 per cent a year and raised the terms of trade by 0.75 per cent a year. Taking the benefits of productivity gains generated by foreign producers through lower prices is a real income gain to Australians.

The second point is that a direct focus on ICTs (and in particular on production) masks the importance of the pre-conditions required to drive the uptake of ICTs. This chapter has emphasised the importance of the incentives provided by competition. Sharper competitive incentives to be productive help to explain why Australia moved from being a technology laggard in previous decades to being at the forefront of new technology uptake in the 1990s. Taking full advantage of declining prices and advances in technologies and not restricting them through trade or other barriers is also conducive to ICT uptake. The development of skills in the workforce can also be important in identifying and developing applications for ICTs.

Strong competition also affects the distribution of productivity gains. A competitive environment means that more of the gains are likely to be passed on in lower prices and thereby assist in dampening inflationary pressures. While the productivity gains appear to be concentrated in a few industries, competition means the benefits are enjoyed by a wider range of industries. Many services, including distribution and financial intermediation, are used extensively by manufacturing and other industries (Simon and Wardrop, 2001). The productivity gains in Wholesaling, even though very large, were passed on, with profit margins declining in the 1990s (Parham *et al.*, 2000). ICT-related or other productivity gains do not in themselves dampen inflation, as some new economy advocates claim. Healthy competition is a necessary pre-condition.

The third and related point is that, especially since ICTs appear (at least thus far) to have generated limited productivity gains in their own right, it is important to foster the factors that are the source of more substantial productivity gains. The USA has enjoyed an MFP acceleration of around 0.3 of a percentage point associated with ICT production and use and other factors. Australia has enjoyed an MFP acceleration of around 1.1 percentage points associated with ICT use—not production—and other factors. To state the obvious, it would be a mistake to focus on chasing a gain of (at most) 0.3 of a percentage point associated with ICTs—especially by concentrating on encouraging ICT production—if that came at the cost of realising a 1.1 percentage point gain from catch-up and 'smart' use of ICTs (where 'smart' implies combining ICTs with complementary product and process innovations, including firm reorganisation).

The Australian experience suggests that the policy priority should be to enhance competition and flexibility in the business environment, rather than focus too strongly or directly on ICTs and the 'new economy'. A focus on the right environmental conditions for business means that the 'smart' productive use of ICTs, and substantial gains unrelated to ICTs, can then follow.

The Australian economy became more focused on productivity and more flexible at just the right time to take advantage of the advances in ICTs that came on stream in the second half of the 1990s. It was not that policymakers deliberately set out with an ICT strategy. Without many predicting or perhaps even realising it, Australia became 'ICT-ready' (and ready for any other technological development that could be usefully employed). Given a history of lagging in the uptake of technology and of relatively poor productivity performance, it is unlikely that Australia would have been as quick on the uptake of ICTs, or as able to use them in productivity-enhancing ways, had it not been for the sea-change that reforms brought.

This is a call for a shift in policy emphasis, rather than a view that few policy implications flow from ICTs and the 'new economy'. Very briefly, ICT-related policy implications include:

- the optimal development of complementary innovations, based on ICTs;
- the optimal development of communications infrastructure;

- the implications of ICT networks for the strength of competition in markets;
- the development of appropriate ICT-related skills;
- adjustment issues concerning job flexibility for those with specific skills displaced by ICTs;
- appropriate protection of intellectual property rights in distribution via the Internet;
- access to networks, including the issue of the 'digital divide';
- regulation of network content; and
- security of tax bases through use of Internet and other networks.

Statistical Needs

Policymakers have a vital interest in productivity growth, as productivity growth is the most important source of improvement in standards of living over the long term.

However, there are no immediate direct productivity 'levers'. Policymakers have to operate indirectly. Understanding the sources and mechanisms of productivity growth helps to set and confirm policy directions.

This chapter has pointed to the importance of a number of statistical issues. Accurate measurement of hedonic prices is undoubtedly difficult in an environment in which characteristics are changing rapidly and in ways that make comparisons over time difficult. But accurate measurement is important in determining the extent of output and productivity growth in ICT production industries and the extent of input growth (and the productivity residual) in ICT-using industries.

There is a related and particularly thorny measurement issue that has not been drawn out in this chapter. This concerns the view that MFP gains specifically associated with advances in ICTs and captured by investors in ICTs (due to product and process innovations contingent upon those advances in ICTs) are mismeasurements and should be factored into the income stream attributable to ICTs. The increased 'usefulness' of ICTs due to technological advances in them should be captured as embodied quality improvements in ICTs. This raises again the issue of the accuracy of allowances for quality changes in forming price deflators.

More information on the sources of productivity improvement at the micro level is needed. There are complexities in the importance of lags in ICT use and interactions with other factors that suggest the need for extensive and reliable longitudinal micro datasets. Data are also needed to investigate the existence and importance of network economies—savings from increasing use of ICT-based networks.

There also needs to be more accurate measurement of output and therefore productivity in service industries, particularly as service industries appear to be the new source of productivity gains. Issues such as convenience, timeliness, accuracy, product range and customisation, as well as new and improved products in a more conventional sense, are looming as even more important measurement issues, in part because of the increased use of ICTs.

The apparent evidence of 'disintermediation' also raises possible measurement issues. For example, some traditional wholesaling activities may have been shifted forward to retailers and backward to manufacturers. Some of the productivity gains, though real, may be misallocated to wholesaling.

In closing, it is worth noting that these statistical issues impinge on the ability of analysts and policymakers to provide some element of detail on the industry sources and mechanisms of productivity growth. However, absence of fully reliable detail does not have to prevent the setting of broad policy directions that centre on competition, openness and flexibility.

Conclusion

Australia has accessed so-called 'new economy' productivity gains associated with ICTs. The gains have been associated with the use of ICTs and not their production. ICT production is not a necessary condition. The lack of a large-scale production sector in Australia, therefore, has not been a barrier to benefiting from ICT-related productivity gains.

Importantly, however, ICT use on its own is not sufficient to generate productivity gains. These come from complementary innovations in products and processes, enabled by the platform that ICTs provide.

The US benchmark suggests that productivity gains associated with 'smart' ICT use are important, but not spectacular, to date — accounting for a few tenths of a percentage point in annual average productivity growth. This may, however, increase in the future. Productivity gains associated with the production of ICTs in the USA have been of a similar order of magnitude. But, while other countries may be able to aspire to similar gains from ICT use as the USA, their ability to generate similar gains from ICT production is much more limited.

For most countries, including Australia, it is better to focus on the strength of competition as an incentive to be more productive, openness to technology transfer and the flexibility of businesses to transform their operations in ways that raise productivity. The Australian experience suggests that the smart use of ICTs, with productivity payoffs (and much larger productivity gains unrelated to ICTs) will then follow. There are also terms of trade gains to be had from importing ICT goods that are declining rapidly in price.

From a policy and productivity point of view, a direct focus on ICTs and the 'new economy' to the exclusion of fostering a competitive, open and flexible business environment would be 'putting the cart before the horse' and would miss a major source of improvement in living standards.

REFERENCES

1. Bean, C. (2000), 'The Australian Economic 'Miracle': A View from the North' in D. Gruen and S. Shrestha (eds), The Australian Economy in the 1990s, *Conference Proceedings, Reserve Bank of Australia*, July.

2. Bresnahan, T., E. Brynjolfsson and L. Hitt, (2002), 'Information Technology, Workplace Organization, and the Demand for Skilled Labour: Firm-level Evidence', *Quarterly Journal of Economics* February:339-376.
3. Brynjolfsson, E. and L. Hitt, (2000), 'Beyond Computation: Information Technology, Organizational Transformation and Business Performance', *Journal of Economic Perspectives* 14(4):23-48.
4. Council of Economic Advisors (2001), *Economic Report of the President*, Transmitted to Congress January 2001, United States Government Printing Office, Washington.
5. Centre for the Study of Living Standards (2000), Trend Productivity and the New Economy, *Paper prepared for the Economic Policy Institute*, September.
6. Dowrick, S. (2000), 'The Resurgence of Australian, Productivity Growth in the 1990s: Miracle or Mirage?', *Paper presented to the 29th Annual Conference of Economists.*
7. Dowrick, S. (2002), 'The Contribution of Innovation and Education to Economic Growth', *Paper presented to the Melbourne Institute and The Australian Conference* 'Towards Opportunity and Prosperity', Melbourne, 4-5 April.
8. Forsyth, P. (2000), 'Microeconomic Policies and Structural Change', pp. 235-267in D. Gruen and S. Shrestha (eds), The *Australian Economy in the 1990s, Conference Proceedings, Reserve Bank of Australia*, 24-25 July.
9. Gordon, R. (2000), 'Does the "New Economy" Measure up to the Great Inventions of the Past?', *Journal of Economic Perspectives* 14(4):49-74.
10. Greenspan, A. (2000a), 'Structural Change in the New Economy', *Remarks to the National Governors' Association, 92nd Annual Meeting*, State College, Pennsylvania, 11 July, http://www.federal reserve.gov/boarddocs/speeches/2000/20000711.htm (accessed on 27 September 2001).
11. Greenspan, A. (2000b), 'Technology, Innovation and Its Economic Impact', *Remarks to the National Technology Forum, St Louis, Missouri*, 7 April, http://www.federalreserve.gov/boarddocs/speeches/2000/20000407.htm (accessed on 27 September 2001).
12. Johnston, A., D. Porter, T. Cobbold and R. Dolamore (2000), Productivity in Australia's Wholesale and Retail Trade,

Productivity Commission Staff Research Paper, AusInfo, Canberra.

13. Jorgenson, D. and K. Stiroh (2000), 'Raising the Speed Limit: US Economic Growth in the Information Age', *Brookings Papers on Economic Activity* 1:125-211.
14. Nordhaus, W. (2001), 'Productivity Growth and the New Economy', *NBER Working Paper 8096.* Cambridge MA, January.
15. OECD (2001a), The New Economy: Beyond the Hype, *The OECD Growth Project*, OECD, Paris.
16. OECD (2001b), OECD *Economic Surveys: Australia*, OECD, Paris.
17. OECD (2001c), *OECD Science, Technology and Industry Scoreboard: Towards a Knowledge-based Economy*, OECD, Paris.
18. Oliner, S. and D. Sichel (2000), 'The Resurgence of Growth in the Late 1990s: Is Information Technology the Story?', *Journal of Economic Perspectives* 14(4):3-22
19. Parham, D. (1999), The New Economy? A New Look at Australia's Productivity Performance, *Productivity Commission Staff Research Paper*, AusInfo, Canberra, May.
20. Parham, D. (2002a), 'Australia's 1990s Productivity Surge and Its Determinants', *Paper presented to the NBER 13th Annual East-Asian Seminar on Economics, Melbourne*, June, (available at http://www.pc.gov.au/research/confproc/prodsurge/index.html).
21. Parham, D. (2002b), 'Productivity Growth in Australia: Are We Enjoying a Miracle', *Paper presented to the Melbourne Institute and The Australian Conference*, 'Towards Opportunity and Prosperity', Melbourne, 4-5 April, (available at http://www.pc.gov.au/research/swp/pgia/index.html).
22. Parham, D., P. Barnes, P. Roberts and S. Kennett (2000), *Distribution of the Economic Gains of the 1990s*, AusInfo, Canberra, November.
23. Parham, D., P. Roberts and H. Sun (2001), Information Technology and Australia's Productivity Surge, *Productivity Commission Staff Research Paper*, AusInfo, Canberra.
24. Productivity Commission (1999), Microeconomic Reforms and Australian Productivity: Exploring the Links, *Commission Research Paper, AusInfo*, Canberra, November.

25. Pilat, D. and F. Lee (2001), 'Productivity Growth in ICT-producing and ICT-using Industries: A Source of Growth Differentials in the OECD?', *STI Working Paper* 2001/4, OECD, Paris.

26. Simon, J. and S. Wardrop (2001), 'Australian Use of Information Technology and Its Contribution to Growth', *Paper prepared for the Conference of Economists*, Perth, September (mimeo).

27. Stiroh, K. (2001), '*Information Technology and the US Productivity Revival: What Do the Industry Data Say*?', Federal Reserve Board of New York (mimeo).

28. Treasury (Commonwealth) (2002), *Budget Papers*, Statement 4: Australia's Terms of Trade—Stronger and Less Volatile, AusInfo, Canberra.

The Importance of ICTs for Developing Countries

According to data from the OCLC Public AVairs Information Service based on a recent European Commission report,[1] a third of the world's population has never made a phone call. This fact emphasises what has become known as the digital divide—the tremendous gap between people with access to information technology (IT), and those without. Not long ago talk of IT to most people signified computers. However, with the rapid and ongoing change in the IT world, computers and communication systems such as telephones and modern fax machines are increasingly using the same technology.

Information and communications technologies (ICTs) is an umbrella term which is currently used to refer to a wide range of services (telephony, fax, internet), applications (such as distance education and management information systems), and technologies (anything from 'old technologies' such as television to 'new technologies' such as cellular phones), using various types of equipment and software, often running over telecoms networks.

The ICT (or information, or communications, or microprocessor) revolution is radically effecting the way we share information about development issues; and governments, NGOs, businesses, institutions, and individuals have jumped on the bandwagon to make ICTs part of their day to day organisational processes. Moreover, the revolution brings leverage in the two essential commodities of time and distance, which in business terms translate into efficiency and cost. The issue of transparency is easier to manage with ICTs, which may result in monetary savings in addition to stakeholder confidence in development processes and systems.

However it is also true that if care is not taken to ensure that ICT provision and use is tailored to the specific needs of the groups that really need them, there is a danger that existing alienation and marginalization will be reinforced and increase.[2]

There is general agreement that ensuring access to the fundamental tools of the digital society is one of the most significant investments the world can make for the future. But the world's most valuable resource is its people. Thus, the significance of ICTs is not in the technologies as such, but in the possibilities they open up for access to knowledge, information, and communications, elements of ever increasing importance in present day economic and social interaction. While some of the issues surrounding ICTs have similarities with those in other areas of infrastructure, such as roads, postal services, and railways, others are of course different and highly specific, with the potential to produce differential development of local and global cultures.

ICTs in the UN context

In this context, in March 2001 the United Nations Economic and Social Council requested the UN Secretary-General to establish an Information and Communication Technologies Task Force. This initiative aims to provide a truly global dimension to the large number of local and regional efforts to bridge the digital divide, to encourage digital opportunity, and to place ICTs at the service of development for all. The Task Force is an innovative mechanism in that it is the first body created by an intergovernmental decision of the UN in which members representing governments, civil society, and organisations of the United Nations system have equal decision-making power. To achieve its goals, the Task Force has set up collaborative links with governments, the private sector, non-pro. T organisations, the academic community, multilateral institutions, and the civil society/NGO community, as well as with other similar initiatives and activities at all levels.[3] It held its inaugural meeting on 19-20 November 2001, at which six thematic working groups were established which were open for participation by non-members of the Task Force.

'ICT for development' is one of the key areas on STD, UNCTAD's internet gateway on science and technology for development.[4] This gateway hosts the homepage of the UN Commission on Science and Technology for Development (UNCSTD), provides continuously updated information on best practice in the assessment, transfer, adaptation, and mastery of technology, and also offers opportunities for partnering and networking in science and technology. On the subject of ICTs, a significant statement was recently made by the Chair of UNCSTD, Professor Vijaya Kumar of Sri Lanka. He made clear that ICTs provide developing countries with an opportunity to increase efficiency in public administration and the business arena, enhance industrial productivity, and promote competitiveness in trade and commerce. However, he also stressed that most developing countries have neither the infrastructure nor the human resources necessary to fully exploit the potential of ICTs. Even where ICT facilities are available, these are often restricted to urban areas and elites, since the costs of ICTs are high when compared with the incomes earned by most inhabitants of developing countries. The digital divide thus not only deprives the poorer developing countries from becoming full and dynamic members of the global economy, it also deprives poorer citizens within these states of the benefits of ICTs.

Various recent international ICT related programmes have been initiated in the context of the UN system. At its fifth session, held in Geneva in 2001, UNCSTD selected as the theme for its intercessional period 2001–2003 'Technology development and capacity-building for competitiveness in a digital society'.[5] The programme for this intercessional period is being carried out by three panels addressing specific aspects of the main theme, with particular attention being given to assimilation and application of ICTs for the purpose of enhancing competitiveness of developing countries and countries with economies in transition. The first of the panels is studying indicators of technological development for 'stocktaking' purposes. The second is exploring the link between foreign direct investment (FDI), technology development for capacity building, and strategic competitiveness. Lastly, the third panel is concentrating on the transfer, diffusion, and use of ICTs.

Technology and Economic Development

The first panel met in Geneva in May 2002 to identify the most important factors affecting technological mastery and development for competitiveness, to attempt to measure them, and to provide a rational explanation of their determinants. In addressing the need for technology indicators, it was decided that countries should be grouped into those that were 'catching up', 'keeping up', and 'getting ahead'. It was agreed that the key objective of collecting a set of indicators was in order to identify policies and programmes. Indicators should not merely be based on economic parameters, but should also include factors concerned directly with scientific and technological development.[6] More specifically, an excellent working document was presented by the secretariat of the UNCSTD, including a comparative analysis of scientific and technological development in around ninety countries in terms of financial resourcing of research (R&D expenditure as a proportion of national income), human capital (enrolments in tertiary education and number of personnel engaged in R&D), as well as export performance (high technology exports as a proportion of total merchandise exports). These various aspects are strongly correlated, with high correlations observed between R&D, human capital, and export performance for the period 1995-99. It was on the basis of the indicators that countries were categorised as 'catching up', 'keeping up', or 'getting ahead', the resulting rankings being reasonably stable over time, though with some regional affects apparent. In general terms, Latin American and transitional economies are classified as 'keeping up', and OECD and some South East Asian countries as 'getting ahead'. This generalisation does however mask substantial variations in countries' experiences, with transitional economies above all showing great differences in all indicators except education and human capital, where they are consistently strong. Data limitations meant that African and South Asian countries had to be largely omitted from this analysis.

Investing in Infrastructure

The second panel, meeting in Sri Lanka in October 2002, paid attention to the strategic use of FDI to transfer technology and to build ICT capabilities. In addition, it examined instruments that could be utilised to achieve 'deep integration' between foreign partners and local firms and suppliers. Finally, the panel also addressed the importance of domestic investment, particularly in R&D and in the ICT infrastructure for improving industrial productivity and enhancing innovation and competitiveness. The main results demonstrate that success in science and technology depends critically on the ability of each system to manage technical change efficiently, and that simply opening up to free trade, investment follows, and external scientific and technological inputs is not an adequate strategy for countries at the low end of the technology ladder.

Evidence from liberalising countries such as Kenya, Tanzania, Zimbabwe, and Ghana shows that after an initial burst of growth, economies with static capabilities slow down as their inherited advantages are exhausted.[7] Without any strategic support from government, they find it difficult to bridge the gap between their skills, technologies, and scientific capabilities and those needed for international competitiveness. This is one important reason why liberalisation has had such poor results in sub-Saharan Africa. Liberalisation has also led to technological regression in many countries of Latin America, with relatively weak growth and competitiveness. The experience of the most successful developing countries in recent economic history (the newly industrialised economies of Asia) suggests that there is a major role for governments in providing the 'collective goods' needed for sustained development. The issue is not *whether* governments should intervene, but *how*.

The third UNCSTD panel, meeting in Angola in January 2003, focussed *Diffusion of ICTs* on transfer and diffusion of ICTs. This panel also examined the extent to which ICTs are being used and diffused in developing countries and how this can affect their ability to 'catch up', 'keep up', and 'get ahead'. The panel formed a picture of the experiences of those countries that have successfully been able to build an indigenous human resource capacity in ICTs, in turn enabling them to become internationally competitive. Nineteen country case studies were reviewed (Czech Republic, Singapore, Indonesia, Vietnam, Uganda, Egypt, Cambodia, Hungary, Bolivia, Nepal, Laos, the Philippines, Malaysia, Thailand, Ethiopia, Morocco, Brazil, Peru, Botswana), as well as ten case studies for e-commerce (Bangladesh, Cambodia, Ethiopia, Madagascar, Mozambique, Myanmar, Nepal, Togo, Uganda, Tanzania).

Besides the activities of the UNCSTD, it is also important to mention the launch in early 2002, by the UN Development Programme (UNDP) in partnership with the Markle Foundation and in consultation with public and private institutions and individual expert partners, of the Global Digital Opportunity Initiative (www.gdoi.org). This initiative is attempting to increase the impact of ICTs in achieving developing countries' development goals by building on the strategic framework developed by the Digital Opportunity Initiative at the 2001 G8 Summit in Genoa, and by working from the fact of nations' growing interdependence. Another significant perspective was provided by the 'measurement' carried out by OECD of the relations between the information economy, ICT sector data, and metadata.[8] In 1998, OECD member countries agreed on a definition of the ICT sector as 'a combination of manufacturing and services industries that capture, transmit and display data and information electronically'. This definition was based on an international standard classification of activities, as a first step towards obtaining some insight into core indicators for the ICT sector. The 1998 activity based definition was reviewed in April 2002, when it was decided that although it gives only a first approximation of the ICT sector, for the moment it should not be changed; instead its implementation should be improved with the aid of more detailed national classifications. This resolution will be reexamined at a later date, in the framework of the major revision of the International Standard Industrial Classification (ISIC) due in 2007.[9]

Use of ICTs to Reduce Inequalities

It is estimated that by 2003 almost all decisions made in science and technology, economics, and business development will be based on information that has been generated electronically. Access to information is thus a key factor in the generation of wealth and there is a strong link between a nation's level of development and the level of technological uptake. Governments are the main actors here, and they need to proceed in partnership with the key stakeholders in ICT provision—including existing and possible future carriers, internet service providers, high technology companies, business users, educators, bankers, and community groups—in order to ensure that a comprehensive system is put in place. Some particular goals for governments include: (*i*) acting as catalysts and giving strong leads in showing the importance of ICT use; (*ii*) creating a regulatory infrastructure to enable easy and effective use of ICTs; (*iii*) establishing genuine and productive partnerships; (*iv*) ensuring that ICTs feature in the mainstream educational curriculum; (*v*) minimizing electronic barriers; (*vi*) taking the needs of poor communities as a starting point, rather than imposing external agenda, ideas, and expectations; (*vii*) facilitating access to scientific and technological information online.

Thus, for example, ICTs can be used to erode inequalities in communications, providing faster and cheaper communication as well as rapid support and advice in times of disaster and emergency. They can also help to reduce oppression and promote human rights by bringing greater attention to bear on individual cases. In the same way, in education ICTs can provide the choice of how, when, where, and at what rate to study, enabling all levels of education to be brought to the more remote parts of the world, and encouraging non-traditional learners to acquire basic literacy skills.

In short, the evidence suggests that under the right conditions ICTs may deliver substantial benefits. However, significant barriers to the effective uptake and use of ICTs by both developed and developing countries also exist, recommending caution in their application. Perhaps, in the end, it may be easier to say what ICTs are not: ICTs are not a magic potion for development or a replacement for real world processes. It seems appropriate to cite the words of UN Secretary-General Kofi Annan during the formal launch of the Task Force on Information and Communications Technology:

The new technologies that are changing our world are not a panacea or a magic bullet. But they are, without doubt, enormously powerful tools for development. They create jobs. They are transforming education, healthcare, commerce, politics, and more. They can help in the delivery of humanitarian assistance and even contribute to peace and security.

REFERENCES

1. 'Information and Communication Technologies in Development: The Role of ICTs in EC Development Policy', European Commission, 2001, europa.eu.int/eur lox/ en/com/cnc/2001/ com2001_0770en01.pdf
2. See for example c. jackson *et al.*: 'Information and Communications Technology and Social Exclusion', *www.student.city.ac.uk/ ~dt758/PrIssuesGroupCoursework.*
3. The Task Force's website is at *www.unicttaskforce.org/about/ principal.asp.*
4. See r0.unctad.org/stdev.

5. 'Technology Development and Capacity-building for Competitiveness in a Digital Society', UNCSTD, 2001, r0.unctad.org/stdev/un/01-03prep.html.
6. See the online database at r0.unctad.org/stdev/database.html.
7. sfilall (ed.): *The TechnologicalResponse to Import Liberalization in Subsaharan Africa*; 1999, New York, NY, St Martin's Press.
8. See *www.oecd.org/EN/countrylist/0,,EN-countrylist-570-1-no-no-1350-0,00.html*
9. For details of the definition, see *www.oecd.org/pdf/M00035000/M00035986.pdf.*

CHAPTER

e-Learning

New Mantra for Distance Education

Introduction

The old correspondence courses were the first Distance Learning courses but with the advent of Internet in the eighties, e-Learning became new mantra for delivering higher education courses over really long distances.

The Internet opened new possibilities and now any type of learning content, be it for school, graduate or masters level, employee training, research activity or any other type of academic offering is called e-Learning. e-Leaning has already established its credentials and its popularity can be gauged from the fact that delivery is not restricted to just plain text but has crossed boundaries to video creating virtual class rooms via video conferencing. The introduction of a variety of technologies has made it possible to convert it from impersonal to highly interactive medium of pedagogy.

Today students feel school is not challenging or interactive enough. It has been said that there are two reasons why we learn; some leaning is essentially forced on us while the other is what we sit back and enjoy. e-Learning has brought back the joy in learning through its innovative and interactive content and delivery.

Need For e-Learning

In the old days, corporate value and value creation were defined principally through material and financial assets. Nowadays a premium is put on intellectual capital. To retain their competitive edge, organizations have started to investigate which training techniques and delivery methods enhance motivation, performance, collaboration, innovation, and a commitment to life-long learning.

The life of knowledge and human skills today is shorter than ever, mounting the pressure to remain up to date with ones education and training throughout a career. In the age of globalization and technological revolution, four-year degrees are just the start of a forty-year continuing education. Life-long learning is quickly becoming an imperative in today's world.

Types of e-Learning

There are fundamentally two types of e-Learning—synchronous training and asynchronous training.

Synchronous

Synchronous, means 'at the same time,' involves interaction of participants with an instructor via the Web in real time.

Asynchronous

Asynchronous, which means 'not at the same time,' allows the participant to complete the WBT at his own pace, without live interaction with the instructor. A new form of learning known as blended learning is emerging. As the name suggests it is an amalgamation of synchronous and asynchronous learning methods.

Asynchronous Methods

Embedded Learning

Embedded learning is information that is accessible on a self-help basis. It can be delivered to the place of work, or to mobile learners. Electronic performance support system (EPSS) is a type of embedded learning. The advantage is that embedded learning offers learners the information they need whenever they need it.

Courses

The clear advantage of a self-paced course is convenience. Participants can get the training they need at any time. This can include just-in-time training where a participant gets exactly the training he or she needs to perform a task.

Discussion Groups

A discussion group is a gathering of conversations that occur over time. They are also called message boards, bulletin boards and discussion forums. Discussion groups can be used to support a group of participants taking the same class or can be used to support participants performing related tasks. A discussion group is a very competent way to supply expert answers to a large group people. A single answer to a common question can help many.

Synchronous Methods

Virtual Classroom

Virtual classroom duplicates the features of a real classroom online. Participants interact with each other and instructors' online, instant messaging, chat, audio and video conferencing etc.

Blended Method

Most institutions prefer to use a mix of both synchronous and asynchronous e Learning methods according to their requirement.

e-Learning in the Future

New varieties of e-Learning have emerged with help and push from emerging technologies. Besides distance learning now there is distributed learning. This term describes the educational experiences of individuals and groups that are distributed over geographies and cultures using variety of media delivery methods.

This has moved education beyond the classroom to more interactive information by joining learning and experience together.

This is developing into learning communities with their own focus on various branches, cultures and sub-cultures. It is a mind boggling explosion of information that is now available with lot of imagination and little effort. With collaborative tools e-Learning is moving into virtual classes and virtual communities where the old methods of practice and test have melted into new interactive teaching-learning methodologies.

Tuition online has taken a new meaning where a varied help is now available both free and paid for on demand on any subject instantly. This has relieved pressure both on the teacher and the students.

Future learning is now focussing on learning beyond the classroom and curriculum. Institutions / Companies need to upgrade employees by offering re-training programmes. These are both costly and time consuming. By designing these programmes and content via e-Learning methods both time and money are saved. The innovative method is also self promoting as it increases the curiosity level of individuals for self promotion and career enhancements.

In the technical field too doctors and other professionals are getting a fair chance for keeping abreast of developments and discoveries and even participation in these activities through interactive delivery processes.

Uses of Blog in e-Learning

Blogging is a personalized, community-linked, social, interactive, innovation built on the distinctive attributes of the Internet. The blogging format includes archives, links, time stamps, chronological listing of thoughts and links.

Blogs are playing a big role in the e-learning environment these days. Instructors as well as learners are using blogs to exchange, communicate and assist in learning. Blogs are increasingly being used by researchers, teachers, and students.

Blogging for Instructors

- Instructors use blogs to post class times and rules, assignment notifications, suggested readings, and exercises and instructional tips for students.
- Blogs are used pass along links and comments about subjects and course announcements and readings.
- Blogs are used to organize in-class discussions and for organizing class seminars.
- Instructors are using blogs to provide summaries of readings and lectures.
- Instructors use blogs for networking and personal knowledge sharing and Knowledge management.
- Blogging also offers speed and the opportunity to interact with diverse viewers both faculty and students globally.

Blogging for Learners

- Blogs are an inventive way for learners to engage in reflective writing on classroom topics.
- Blogs provide information dissemination, and provide learners with the opportunity to present his or her thoughts and opinions.
- Blogs provide individual feedback to the learners from instructors.
- Blogs are great for disusing ideas, experiences or opinions and allow learners to discuss publicly what they are studying with other students and experts globally.
- Blogging is helping learners to think and write more critically, learners tend to research and study harder when blogs are used.

Conclusion

e-Learning has created a new dimension in education, both within and beyond the curriculum and is still looking at further opportunities of becoming more useful via new emerging technologies. We are really on the threshold of new opportunities and this is just the beginning of a new horizon of education. There are millions of blogs on the web, hosted both by instructors and learners alike, they present an opportunity for anyone and everyone to join in the e-Learning revolution which is being increase blog by blog.

REFERENCES

1. Bates, Tiny (2001), National Strategies for e-Learning in Post Secondary Education and Training—Paris, UNESCO.
2. Rosenberg, Marc Jeffy (2001), e-Learning, New York, McGraw-Hill.
3. Satheeshkumar (2008), e-Learning Possibilities in Education, Neelkamal Publication, Hyderabad.
4. Vandana Gupta (2008), e-Learning Pedagogies New Approaches to Teaching and Assessment, Neelkamal Publication, Hyderabad.

CHAPTER

Impact of ICTs in Rural Areas

"It is a revolution that is happening here! Villagers and women at that, proving to the world that technology are not alien to them. This is the way forward."

—*Dr. Specioza Wandira Kazibwe,*
Former Vice President, Republic of Uganda

Context—Why is This Project Important?

The evolution of information and communication technologies (ICTs) in India has created a technological divide between the 'haves' and the 'have-nots.' As many of India's companies and well-educated enjoy the benefits of ICTs, these technologies are still not accessible or affordable for the majority of the population. The divide is exacerbated by the deeply ingrained disparities of gender and social class, which determine who can or cannot use technology. Despite recent deregulation and decentralization within India since the 1990s, which has strengthened the voice of the poor and the role of NGOs, there remains widespread poverty. Development initiatives, especially in rural areas, are hampered by weaknesses in technological infrastructure. Accessibility is also hindered by language barriers, and a lack of suitable content and applications in local languages.

The Project—How Does This Initiative Address the Development Problem?

Pan Asia's collaboration with the M.S. Swaminathan Research Foundation began in 1997, with the first phase of Impact of ICTs in Rural Areas. This phase aimed to assess and document the impact of ICTs in fostering sustainable agricultural and rural development and bridging the gap between the 'haves' and the 'have-nots.' During the first phase of the project, seven village knowledge centers (VKCs) were established in the rural areas of the Union Territory of Pondicherry. The second phase began in 2001, with additional funding from CIDA (Canadian International Development Agency), and has since established 4 more VKCs and deployed ICTs more widely throughout the region. The goal of this phase was to enhance connectivity in rural Pondicherry, and to assess the potential sustainability of the project.

The project used a hub-and-spokes model, whereby one village knowledge centre, operated by project staff, acts as a central hub for communication with the 11 other knowledge centers in surrounding villages as the spokes. Encouraging community ownership by involving the many local actors, including public and private partners and village volunteers, enhanced the project's sustainability. The program challenged traditional gender roles by recruiting mainly women as volunteers for the centers. The project was designed to be non-discriminatory in its delivery of services, and provides relevant local information in Tamil language, both in written and verbal formats. As such, availability and accessibility for everyone is ensured. In addition to encouraging communal ownership of and access to ICTs in rural communities, *Impact of ICTs in Rural Areas* created an important knowledge base about how ICTs can best be used to further development in rural areas.

A third phase of the project titled 'Impact of ICTs on Poverty Alleviation in Rural Pondicherry' was approved in 2004, which focuses on ascertaining whether or not new, innovative ICTs can bring better economic sustainability to the existing project; while at the same time, contribute to further improvements in the education and health sector. The social and economic impacts of ICTs are assessed systematically through surveys, interviews, and participatory rural appraisal techniques to determine their effectiveness in poverty alleviation in rural Pondicherry. This phase specifically utilizes and assesses the following technologies: wireless fidelity (WiFi); 2.5G mobile technology (includes mobile telephones enabled to transmit data via General Packet Radio Service); Global Positioning System (GPS) for fisher people to improve knowledge of fishing zones and potential ocean hazards; Voice over Internet Protocol (VoIP) for low-cost long distance voice communication; and RailTel, a village network backbone via the Government of India-backed broadband network across India's railway networks. Some of the ICT-based programs being implemented in the villages include the development of an ICT-enabled integrated health system, computer-assisted learning centers for rural children, a multimedia indigenous knowledge directory for Pondicherry, a web-based information on food security, and a training course in knowledge management for local women. MSSRF is also experimenting with the use of open source software. The experience of this research project will be integrated into the National Virtual Academy for Food Security and Rural Prosperity, a new initiative of the MSSRF for ending hunger and eradicating rural poverty in India.

Objectives

To assess the impact and sustainability of programs for the use of ICTs in rural areas of India. More specifically, the project aimed to:

- Develop a set of parameters to make a choice of access technology and technology for powering the access devices
- Organise workshops and other interactions such as on-site consultations with policy makers to sensitise them to critical issues in the use of ICTs to promote human development in rural areas
- Fully transfer ownership of the project-supported rural telecentres from the project to rural communities to be completed within the timeframe of the project

- Develop ICT-based applications for rural areas, especially community banking online and distance education, to assess their potential to contribute to the sustenance of a rural ICT programme
- Conduct research on formation of multi-sectoral partnerships (private-public/government-NGOs) with rural communities to form a sustainable model of ICTs for rural areas
- Exchange research results with telecentre programmes in different parts of the world, to arrive at a more comprehensive picture of impact assessment and sustainability issues and its possible internalization in project implementation

Development Impact

The project was able to provide several types of ICTs and ICT-based services to 12 different villages in the Union Territory of Pondicherry, and furthermore critically consider the advantages and disadvantages of each of these technologies. The technologies provided and assessed include: VHF Duplex radios, spread spectrum technology, satellite based internet connectivity, public address systems, and a community newspaper. Surprisingly, the newspaper was especially successful in creating awareness of and interest in the community knowledge centers, and in providing a forum in which villagers could publish news and concerns related specifically to development issues within their own community. Within two days of the release of the newspaper's first issue, the program received over 60 phone calls from villagers interested in their services. The technology provided to these rural communities has directly saved lives. Residents of Nallavadu, Pondicherry, survived the recent tsunami that devastated the area thanks to technology that MSSRF established with support from the IDRC. When one of the village residents received a phone call warning her of the approaching tsunami, she and her neighbours were able to broadcast the news across the village using a loudspeaker system that had been installed by MSSRF to inform fishermen of the water conditions. The entire village, more than 3,500 individuals, was able to evacuate in time to survive the tsunami.

The project held several workshops aimed at promoting awareness of ICTs and their uses in development, and at gaining input from the communities and policy makers involved. The first such workshop was held in October 2003 and another one the following year. These Policy Makers Workshops resulted in the creation of a National Alliance entitled "Mission 2007: Every Village a Knowledge Centre." This movement involves members of the private sector, cooperatives, non-governmental organizations, research and development institutions, women's associations, mass media, and appropriate government agencies in the mission to establish a knowledge centre in each of India's 600,000 villages by the year 2007, the 60th anniversary of the nation's independence.

The program has provided training to knowledge centre volunteers on basic computer applications and volunteers, in turn, have trained tens of thousands of their neighbours. In 2003 alone, over 10,000 individuals were trained on computers through village knowledge centers. Software has also been developed to train the villagers in micro-enterprise and to assist self-help groups in managing their funds. These tools, combined with training on non-technological skills such as making ornamental artifacts from shells, has helped fishing village members, especially women, to alleviate some of the economic hardship faced during the annual 45 day fishing ban. Not only has the program benefited the villages of the Union Territory of Pondicherry, but it has produced a great wealth of information that can be exchanged with other programs with similar objectives. One of the program's initiatives is the annual South-South Exchange Traveling Workshop on ICT-enabled development, bringing together participants from different countries of Africa and Asia. African participants in the workshop were inspired to initiate a few programs in their own countries based on what they learned. *Impact of ICTs in Rural Areas* was also able to learn from suggestions made during the workshop, and has since formed women self help groups in Nallavadu, based on an observation by workshop participants regarding lack of female participation in local government.

Global Trends in ICT and Education

In the spirit of the new year and all things dealing with resolutions and lists, I submit below my first blog posting for the EduTech blog (checking off a resolution) with a discussion of 10 Global Trends in ICT and Education for 2010 and beyond (joining the crowded space of lists in this new year). The list is an aggregation of projections from leading forecasters such as the *Horizon Report*, personal observations and a good dose of guesswork. The Top 10 Global Trends in ICT and Education are:

1. **Mobile Learning:** New advances in hardware and software are making mobile "smart phones" indispensable tools. Just as cell phones have leapfrogged fixed line technology in the telecommunications industry, it is likely that mobile devices with internet access and computing capabilities will soon overtake personal computers as the information appliance of choice in the classroom.
2. **Cloud computing:** Applications are increasingly moving off of the stand alone desk top computer and increasingly onto server farms accessible through the Internet. The implications of this trend for education systems are huge; they will make cheaper information appliances available which do not require the processing power or size of the PC. The challenge will be providing the ubiquitous connectivity to access information sitting in the 'cloud'.
3. **One-to-One computing:** The trend in classrooms around the world is to provide an information appliance to every learner and create learning environments that assume universal access to the technology. Whether the hardware involved is one laptop per child (OLPC), or—increasingly—a net computer, smart phone, or the re-emergence of the *tablet,* classrooms should prepare for the universal availability of personal learning devices.

4. **Ubiquitous learning:** With the emergence of increasingly robust connectivity infrastructure and cheaper computers, school systems around the world are developing the ability to provide learning opportunities to students "anytime, anywhere". This trend requires a rethinking of the traditional 40 minute lesson. In addition to hardware and Internet access, it requires the availability of virtual mentors or teachers, and/or opportunities for peer to peer and self-paced, deeper learning.
5. **Gaming:** *A recent survey by the Pew Internet and American Life Project* per the Horizon Report found that massively multiplayer and other online game experience is extremely common among young people and that games offer an opportunity for increased social interaction and civic engagement among youth. The phenomenal success of games with a focus on active participation, built in incentives and interaction suggests that current educational methods are not falling short and that educational games could more effectively attract the interest and attention of learners.
6. **Personalized learning:** Education systems are increasingly investigating the use of technology to better understand a student's knowledge base from prior learning and to tailor teaching to both address learning gaps as well as learning styles. This focus transforms a classroom from one that teaches to the middle to one that adjusts content and pedagogy based on individual student needs—both strong and weak.
7. **Redefinition of learning space:** The ordered classroom of 30 desks in rows of 5 may quickly become a relic of the industrial age as schools around the world are re-thinking the most appropriate learning environments to foster collaborative, cross-disciplinary, students centered learning. Concepts such as greater use of light, colors, circular tables, individual spaces for students and teachers, and smaller open learning spaces for project-based learning are increasingly emphasized.

8. **Teacher-generated open content:** OECD school systems are increasingly empowering teachers and networks of teachers to both identify and create the learning resources that they find most effective in the classroom. Many online texts allow teachers to edit, add to, or otherwise customize material for their own purposes, so that their students receive a tailored copy that exactly suits the style and pace of the course. These resources in many cases complement the official textbook and may, in the years to come, supplant the textbook as the primary learning source for students. Such activities often challenge traditional notions of intellectual property and copyright.
9. **Smart portfolio assessment:** The collection, management, sorting, and retrieving of data related to learning will help teachers to better understand learning gaps and customize content and pedagogical approaches. Also, assessment is increasingly moving toward frequent formative assessments which lend itself to real-time data and less on high-pressure exams as the mark of excellence. Tools are increasingly available to students to gather their work together in a kind of online portfolio; whenever they add a tweet, blog post, or photo to any online service, it will appear in their personal portfolio which can be both peer and teacher assessed.
10. **Teacher managers/mentors:** The role of the teacher in the classroom is being transformed from that of the font of knowledge to an instructional manager helping to guide students through individualized learning pathways, identifying relevant learning resources, creating collaborative learning opportunities, and providing insight and support both during formal class time and outside of the designated 40 minute instruction period. This shift is easier said than done and ultimately the success or failure of technology projects in the classroom hinge on the human factor and the willingness of a teacher to step into unchartered territory.

These trends are expected to continue and to challenge many of the delivery models fundamental to formal education as it is practiced in most countries. It will be interesting to reflect back on this list at the end of the year to see which ideas have gained the most traction; and what new ideas will make a list for 2011....

In 2010 we welcome a new blogger to the team! Robert Hawkins is a Sr. Education Specialist in the World Bank with a focus on science and technology as well as the role of technology in education.

How will ICT Change the Future of Education?

Educators from Malaysia, Australia and India foresee a future in which digital books, hybrid mobile computers and touch-screen writing tablets will replace the text book, chalk and blackboard, according to a series of interviews in the FutureGov magazine on how technology will change the future of education. Emeritus Professor Jonathan Anderson, Flinders University of South Australia, predicts that knowledge in the form of books and printed matter will rapidly become digitised. Today, full text of over seven million books can be accessed through Google Books. This number is growing quickly as Google expands its digitisation effort with international associations, publishers and authors. Companies such as Amazon.com and Sony are also contributing to this development.

Many libraries in Asia Pacific are aggressively digitising content. The National Library in Kolkata—the largest library in India—is going through a massive digitisation effort. "We have digitised 9140 books and converted close to 180,000 records into machine-readable formats last year," said Asesh Ghatak, Library and Information Officer, National Library, Belvedere, Kolkata in India. New mobile devices will emerge and take on a great role in the way students learn. "We are likely to see a convergence of mobile and PC technologies as rival chip manufacturers enter each other's territory," explained Anderson. He predicted that smart phones will become more like computers and vice versa.

Dr Norrizan Razali, Senior Manager, Smart School Department, Multimedia Development Corporation in Malaysia agreed. "One of the key emerging technologies that will transform schools is mobile devices. Hybrid devices which are a mix of mobile phones and personal notebooks," she added. Razali believed that such a mobile device will make a great impact to students, especially in rural Malaysia. However, it must first be durable and affordable—below RM 1000 (US$292) each.

The increasing pervasiveness of cloud computing will support such a device. Cloud enables operating systems to be trimmed down and applications to rely less on end-clients for processing power and memory space. Also, touch-screen technology will become the key method students interact with ICT devices. "Such a device will be held in the hand like a mobile phone but it will have a larger surface, something like a writing tablet. It will be used for all kinds of communicating—browsing the internet, emailing, reading books and other materials online, phoning and texting, and social networking with friends and colleagues," Anderson elaborated.

Social networking sites such as Facebook and Twitter will continue to rule students' time. According to a recent Australian study, Facebook was the fourth most visited site. On average, users spend an average of 26.5 hours each week online, and a quarter of that time—6.5 hours—is dedicated to Facebook. Visits to Twitter increased 1000 per cent compared to the year before.

While it is not easy to spell out the implications for education, Anderson advised that educators need to keep abreast of the latest ICT developments and echoed the need for teachers to be brought up to speed on new technology.

Index

J

K

L

M

N